THE PHILOSOPHY OF BRANDING

With thanks to Pauline, Barbara and Pierre

THE PHILOSOPHY OF BRANDING

Great Philosophers
Think Brands

Thom Braun

**KOGAN
PAGE**

London and Sterling, VA

First published in Great Britain and the United States in 2004 by Kogan Page Limited
Reprinted 2004

120 Pentonville Road
London N1 9JN
UK
www.kogan-page.co.uk

22883 Quicksilver Drive
Sterling VA 20166-2012
USA

© Thom Braun, 2004

ISBN 0 7494 4193 3

British Library Cataloguing-in-Publication Data

A CIP record for this book is available from the British Library.

Library of Congress Cataloging-in-Publication Data

Braun, Thom, 1953-
  The philosophy of branding : great philosophers think brands / Thom Braun.
    p. cm.
  ISBN 0-7494-4193-3
1. Brand name products–Philosophy. 2. Business names–Philosophy. 3. Product management–Philosophy. I. Title.
HD69.B7B74 2004
658.8'27'01–dc22
                          2003028084

Typeset by Jean Cussons Typesetting, Diss, Norfolk
Printed and bound in Great Britain by Biddles Ltd, King's Lynn, Norfolk

Contents

By way of introduction

Socrates and Wittgenstein sat themselves down on a garden bench so as to be able to continue the conversation more comfortably.

Socrates: As I understand it, the book is an introduction to what some of the greatest Western philosophers have had to say about brands, branding and brand management. Is that not an interesting point from which to investigate such an important aspect of marketing?

Wittgenstein: No, it's clearly an absurd proposition – a statement without meaning. We all know that the philosophers referred to wrote not one word about the subject of brands.

Socrates: In one sense, at least, you are right, of course. But it is surely a matter of interpretation. The author has admittedly taken a few liberties with what the philosophers actually said or wrote.

Wittgenstein: Liberties! The simple truth is that none of the people he writes about had a philosophy of branding. Branding did not exist in any meaningful sense during the times that most of them lived. And, even if it *had* done, the individuals cited would certainly not have wasted any of their thought on such a subject.

Socrates: That is again a matter of interpretation. If we start by assuming that brands and branding touch something deep and fundamental in human beings – the need to identify, and identify *with*, things, for example – then we will come to a different conclusion. The point is surely that if the philosophers *had* considered the subject, then they might well have expressed their thoughts in the ways set out in this book.

Wittgenstein: Even accepting your premise, the idea that brands and branding should be approached through philosophical investigation is obscure, if not esoteric. I cannot believe that any right-thinking brand manager would ever consider such a preciously academic approach to what is clearly a matter of business. All of which supports my hypothesis that the book is without meaning.

Socrates: No, my friend, the book is far from being academic or obscure. Its point is, indeed, very simple. It is to suggest that all modern, complex and apparently sophisticated approaches to brands and branding must be grounded in a rigorous and, yes, philosophical view of the way the world works.

Wittgenstein: But why philosophy? Both you and I know that 'philosophy' can be defined in a number of ways, but that it is always basically a single-minded and rational investigation of being, knowledge and right conduct. What can that investigation have to do with branding?

Socrates: A great deal, I would suggest. The things you mention all lie at the heart of brands and branding in some shape or form. The book simply uses 'philosophy' to draw out a series of fundamental principles for the development and management of brands – all based on the thoughts of some of the greatest of Western minds. Including yours, of course.

The smile that played around Socrates' mouth only served to irritate his colleague all the more. Wittgenstein made a growling sound, stood up, and stomped heavily back up the garden path.

PART I

All Greek to me

To all intents and purposes, Western philosophy began with the Ancient Greeks. So too did branding. To be more precise, several of the concepts we use today in the context of brands and branding were created by the great minds of the ancient world.

Socrates was the first philosophy superstar – but he was certainly not the first to think his way around the subject. The so-called pre-Socratics made important contributions to the philosophy of branding – and key among them was Heraclitus. That's where we begin.

Socrates, of course, put his own special stamp on the

way the subject developed, and he was followed closely by Plato and then by Aristotle. Between them they laid the foundations for all philosophical thought over the next two thousand years. And, in doing so, they created a base for the way a 'philosophy of branding' was to evolve.

The four thinkers covered in Part I made clear for the first time:

- the changing nature of the world in which brands have to exist;
- the importance of rigorously questioning everything about a brand;
- the relationship between a brand's superficial qualities and its deeper, more lasting nature;
- the need to maintain a focus on the functional elements of a brand (what it *does*).

1 Heraclitus – and the place from where we start

Heraclitus (c. 540–475 BC) was born at Ephesus, in what is now Turkey. He is grouped together with several other early Greek thinkers under the heading 'pre-Socratics' – on the basis that Western philosophy, as we commonly define it, dates from Socrates (see Chapter 2).

Heraclitus said 'A hidden connection is stronger than an obvious one.' The connection between Philosophy and Branding is certainly not obvious – but is arguably strong. Certainly Heraclitus sets us well on the way to uncovering some (perhaps hidden) nuggets of good brand thinking.

Probably Heraclitus's greatest perception was that the world is continually in flux. Nothing is stable. Everything changes constantly.

Now this probably sounds unsurprising to the 21st-century ear. We may even regard it as a cliché. We are surely all used to change – and even more used to being *told* that we live in a time of change. At one level at least, change is something we take for granted.

But Heraclitus was not simply talking about change in relative terms. He was talking about change as inherent in the nature of everything all the time.

In this respect, anything that is in existence is not the same from one moment to the next. He pointed out that it is not possible to step into the same river twice. Whilst this may be fairly obvious, it is also profound. (Which is the case with much of the philosophy we'll consider.)

It should also make us realize that what we regularly label 'change' (a new home, a new job or relationship) is easy to identify compared to the total and sometimes imperceptible flux that is the world.

A matter of flux

This state of flux applies to *everything*.

Now, when Heraclitus said everything – given that he was talking about *continual* flux – he was including everything that was *then*, and everything that was about to be. And so on. Right up to now. And past now. Forever. If you see what I mean. Which clearly includes all our modern notions of marketing and consumer branding.

Any 'thing', at any stage in history, is not a stable entity. It is merely something in transition. Heraclitus's best-known metaphor for describing this was the flame. A flame may be a 'thing' – but, in an important sense, it is not the *same* thing from one moment to another. When we look at a flame we are witnessing a process.

Again, this may seem obvious. But at another level, it is not. Much of the time we think and talk about our world, and the 'things' in it, as if they were permanent – or at least as things which are stable for periods of time. How else could we measure things, make plans, have expectations, live from one day to the next – unless there were a guaranteed level of stability in the world?

Against that view, Heraclitus reminds us of the transience of things – including ourselves. That recognition should stop us from talking glibly of 'a changing world'. The fact is, the world is in constant flux. There is quite literally nothing we can do to live outside of that flux.

What does that mean for brands and branding?

Why brands?

Brand marketers are used to talking about brands as things that provide reference points for consumers in an ever-changing world. The logic goes something like this. The rate of change and innovation is so great, and the number of conflicting media messages about what is good for us so overwhelming, that we need a kind of shorthand to help us tell the good from the not-so-good.

Brands help us to do that. They act as signposts in a busy marketplace, clustering values and characteristics together in recognizable packages that we regard with different levels of trust or approval. Brands *stand* for something – and, as we all know, what they stand *for* often goes much further than superficial product or service attributes.

Here's an example. I know (well, I don't – but I take it on trust) that a BMW (any BMW) is a good car – well engineered, safe, and so on. However, I wouldn't want one. Why? Because every BMW has 'wannabee' written all over it. It's a car for people who think they've made it to a certain level, think they're on course for the next level, and want to tell everyone about it.

Now that's nothing to do with the car itself, of course – but everything to do with the brand. Because the *brand* is what exists inside my head, and not what is parked in front of your house.

OK, that's a rather sweeping judgement – and at one fell swoop I've probably alienated a large proportion of the people who started to read this book. But the example has a point.

I *used* to have a BMW. It was a long time ago. A lovely car. Everyone thought so. Especially the wannabee car thieves. It was broken into every other week. (Slight exaggeration – but you know what I mean.)

But things move on. Back to the flux.

All inside my head – and yours

BMW have been fantastically consistent in the way they have built and nurtured the brand. Yes, of course, it has evolved in the years since I owned one. Product, advertising, positioning to some extent. But, overall, it has remained largely true to itself. You might say the flux in the car market has been well managed by the brand. So what has changed in my relationship with BMW?

The answer is pretty simple. Clearly the flux in *me* has been the telling factor. And, as I've already said – and will continue to repeat – there is only one place where a brand exists. Inside consumers' heads (and possibly hearts – but more of that later). In this case, inside *my* head.

So what has Heraclitus got to do with this? In his little-known teachings on consumer branding, Heraclitus said that we (brand developers and managers of one kind or another) must start from a point that assumes that everything is in flux all the time.

Any semblance of stability is simply an illusion, a mirage. Brands are in no way any more inherently stable than anything else in the world. In fact, the opposite is true. They are far *less* stable, because (again) the only place they exist is in the heads of their current and potential consumers.

Now, when Heraclitus said this, he threw down a fundamental challenge about first principles to the early brand marketers of Ephesus around the year 500 BC. They were pretty much in agreement that brand management was about creating, developing, building and maintaining *things* (brands) which had a substance, a relevance and a reality that went beyond the limitations of natural life. They saw brands a bit like the rather impressive buildings their architect colleagues were putting up all over the place. Yes, they took a while to build – but once up, they stood a fair chance of lasting for several lifetimes. Brands were surely the same.

Some brand marketers think like this today. It is all too easy to assume that brands are, or should be, fixed points in a changing world. But this can only be true in part. And it's a very dangerous assumption to start from.

A much healthier starting point is Heraclitus. So, to summarize ...

Don't blink – or you'll miss it

Branding, and especially brand development, is often portrayed as being about the creation of stability and consistency in a sea of change. Brands as signposts in an uncertain world.

That may be an *outcome* of successful brand development – but it's not where the brand developer should start. She or he should start by recognizing that brands are no more stable than the very unstable world in which they exist. They must be developed and managed on that basis.

As a brand marketer you can't afford to take your

eye off your brand for a minute. You have to assume that it will, in some way or another, be different tomorrow to the way it is today. Not necessarily because of anything that *you* have done – but because something else has changed in the world of flux, and in the consumer's head. A new trend, a competitor move, a different expectation or aspiration, a sudden change in fashion, a startling scientific discovery, a scurrilous press report, a totally unexpected and unforeseeable 'paradigm shift'. The possibilities are endless – and just because you haven't spotted them doesn't mean they're not there, changing things as we speak. As you read this page. Right now, this minute!

Just as you can't step in the same river twice, you will not be developing the same brand in the same market two days running. Now at one level I know that sounds absurd. Yes, of course you have to make *some* assumptions, otherwise you can't do *any*thing. Just as we have to assume that the sun will rise tomorrow – except that (as we'll see later) philosophically there is no reason at all why we *should* make that assumption. (The fact that it has risen every day since the dawning of time is absolutely no guarantee that it will rise tomorrow.)

But, putting that aside for a moment, you have to start by assuming that all bets are off. The world is flux, and there is nothing you can take for granted.

That's where the modern brand marketer has to start. And it's Heraclitus we have to thank for that.

Heraclitus's top tip

Assume that nothing is stable in the world in which your brand exists. Everything is always changing all the time. The relative position and perception of your brand will not be the same from one day to the next. It therefore has to be managed on the basis of constant flux.

---

2 Socrates – and the art of questioning

So much for the chatty opening chapter. Now on to the heavy stuff.

Of the five or six most significant, and perhaps most famous, philosophers of the Western world, three are Ancient Greeks. And the first of these is Socrates.

Socrates was the father of philosophy as we most commonly define it. Before Socrates, the early Greek philosophers concentrated most of their thought on the nature of the world. In that respect, philosophy was the 'science' of the day: it dealt largely with how things were made, and how they fitted together.

Socrates turned the focus of attention away from the

world as such, and onto humankind. In effect, the philosophy of Socrates was moral philosophy – and its central concern was an understanding of the motivations on which we act.

Socrates was born in Athens about 470 BC. His lifetime coincided with what has become known as the golden age of Athens – a period which saw the city at the height of its influence politically and culturally. In an environment of clever and accomplished men in every field of intellectual endeavour, Socrates stood out as someone special. Yet he was a man who seems to have been quite unexceptional in his appearance, and who left behind him not one page of written philosophy. Why, therefore, was he so influential then – and why does he remain so now?

His pivotal position at the centre of the intellectual life of Athens must have been due to an extraordinarily charismatic presence. Perhaps no philosopher since has come close to holding the personal sway that Socrates enjoyed. The fact that his influence has remained so strong to this day is due to the clarity of his method, and the uncompromising positions to which such a method is bound to lead. Indeed, his death (of which more later) was a direct result of this principled and unswerving adherence to 'truth'.

The fact that we know anything at all about what

Socrates said and stood for is all due to Plato (see Chapter 3), who recorded much of his master's teaching. So what was at the heart of that teaching?

Questions, questions – nothing but questions

Two key things drive Socrates' thought overall – persistent questioning in pursuit of 'truth', and an unrelenting focus on the way our understanding of 'truth' affects our behaviour. Those thoughts are also at the heart of his philosophy of branding.

Not many people nowadays know that Socrates ran branding workshops. Well, sort of. Philosophical seminars might be another term for them.

While at one level they were clearly the fore-runners of our modern-day branding workshops, in various key dimensions they differed profoundly from the kinds of events experienced by 21st-century brand marketers. The key difference – at least superficially – was that they were *not* characterized by walls covered in sheets of paper from the ubiquitous flip-chart.

There were three reasons for this:

1. The workshops were held outdoors, so there were no walls.

2. Flip-charts had not been invented.
3. Socrates wrote nothing down – and neither did he encourage the workshop participants to write anything. (Which goes a long way to explaining why the branding workshops in particular still remain relatively unknown.)

Instead of so-called creativity sessions, anarchic brainstorming, and frantic scribbling on flip-charts, Socrates' workshops revolved around *questions*. This may seem either obvious or trite – but the fact is that, in the development of brand and branding strategies, we often lose sight of the need for rigour and the positive use of constant questioning.

Sound familiar?

How often have you been to a brand workshop where the branding or advertising agency begins one of its set-piece brainstorming techniques aimed at generating a set of brand values. An hour later the flip-chart is full of the same old words – almost regardless of the brand or the market in which you happen to be working. It could be cars, coffee, telecoms, or contraceptives – the words on the flip-chart invariably end up being the same.

Quality, Integrity, Value, Relationship, Accessibility, Trust, Relevance, Responsibility, User-Friendliness.

I could go on. The very worst workshops of this kind are the ones where the list is compiled and then simply stuck up on the wall, so that it glowers back at you for the rest of the day.

The slightly (but only slightly) better workshops go through the same initial stages, and then move on in the following way. The agency facilitator thanks everyone for their brainstorming contributions, but then points out that none of the generated values is at all discriminating versus the competition.

The workshop then launches itself into a second round of brainstorming, and finally (in sheer desperation) fixes on values which appear to be differentiated simply because no one else in this particular market sector has had the foresight to use them. You know the sort of thing ... the bank that decides it's going to be Sexy, Fast, & Customer-Focused.

Needless to say, these exercises don't get you very far. They stir up a lot of hot-air and sometimes excitement on the day, but they very rarely help build your brand.

Socrates' workshops were quite different. Socrates fully accepted that values like Quality, Integrity, Value, and so on, all had to be a part of most brands. What was important, however, was not to dismiss them therefore as generic – but rather to probe to a deeper level of understanding. What was needed was an interrogation of the so-called values in the context of the brand and market in question.

Getting under the skin

So, right … Integrity is important for a brand. So what do we mean by Integrity? What *is* Integrity? What is it in this context? In this market? For this brand? For this particular set of consumers?

Now that in itself may sound unexceptional: we all ask questions all the time. But we probably don't do it explicitly, publicly, or with a real sense of method and purpose. Whereas Socrates did.

Not only did he question doggedly, acutely, and persistently: he did it all in the relentless pursuit of 'truth' – by which he mostly meant the real motivational base that drives us to behave in the way that we do. It is for this reason that we refer to his philosophy largely as 'moral philosophy'.

If the starting point is persistent questioning – of the branding context, consumers, ideas, the brand itself – the end point has to be a change in behaviour. If behaviour is not changed, nothing has been achieved.

At his workshops Socrates challenged the Athenian

marketing and brand managers who thought they already knew the truth about themselves, their consumers, and their brands. But Socrates was not merely trying to uncover 'truth' on a case-by-case basis. He was first and foremost a teacher and a coach. His aim was not simply to solve individual brand problems, but rather to change first the way people *thought* – and, on that basis, how they then acted. And he did this by encouraging all the Athenian brand marketers who came under his sway to question *every*thing, and to take nothing for granted.

It was a whole new way of thinking, and it established the model for a process we now think of as *dialectic.* This forces people to interrogate what they think they already know (current 'truth') via a rigorous process of question and answer.

There is an important point to be made here, however, which is that, for this approach to work well, it needs to be undertaken within a brand and company culture that welcomes challenge, and is supportive of 'going deeper'.

Who mentioned 'culture'?

Not every business will be comfortable with a Socratically minded brand manager who questions everything all the time in the search for 'truth'. Sometimes it's easier to nod at the bland flip-chart, and then move on.

And then there are those businesses where questioning is a normal part of the business culture – but where it is almost entirely used in a negative and often destructive way. (Beware the apparently Socratic veneer beneath which lurks the second-rate mind that asks questions only because it is incapable of joined-up thinking.)

The genuine Socratic method of brand thinking only works if undertaken in a company culture that really does want to get to the heart of the matter – as a basis for action that is better and more effective, because it is aligned to, and derived from, the 'truth'.

Rigorous questioning – of the values, motivations, and perceptions of all the brand's stakeholders – is fundamental to good branding and brand management. But if your company culture is not used to this kind of interrogation, then you might easily make yourself very unpopular.

Socrates himself was adored by many, but regarded by others as a subversive. Several prominent Athenian marketing directors, among others, took exception to the way their brand managers started to question everything around them.

This ultimately led to Socrates' arrest. He was charged with corrupting the young men of the city, tried and condemned to death. In ancient Athens, the condemned had to take poison themselves or be killed, and in 399 BC, when he was about 70 years old, Socrates took hemlock and died.

In many respects Socrates became one of Western civilization's two or three most famous martyrs for 'the truth'.

In all areas of life his approach is as relevant now as it was then. It is an approach that insists that everything must be subject to questioning – indeed that 'truth' cannot be uncovered without such an interrogation. And it should remind us of the fundamental importance of rigour in the way we seek to define our brand values and branding strategies.

Socrates' top tip

Question everything – literally everything – about your brand. Take nothing for granted. Always look to get to a deeper level of understanding. And don't settle for anything that doesn't feel like 'the truth'.

3 Plato – and seeing below the surface

The pre-Socratics, and Heraclitus in particular, pointed to the complexities that make up our world. Socrates, through his sheer strength of character and clarity of thinking, focused the debate on what we might call 'moral philosophy'. Both teach us something important about branding: first, the need to deal with constant change and flux in the world, and secondly the need to pin down some basic reference points through a relentless and restless questioning of everything around us.

Neither, however, approached a theory of brands and branding as such. That was left to Plato, arguably the greatest and (in the long term) probably the most influential of the Ancient Greek philosophers.

Plato's starting point was Socrates. Plato was the pupil of Socrates, and almost everything we know of the teacher's work and words we know through the writings of his most distinguished acolyte. Plato is quite unique within the group of Greeks we are considering here because history has preserved all his main original texts. Not only are we blessed by having such an extensive collection of his thinking, but (importantly) all Plato's works are easy to read in translation. (Which is more than can be said for a number of the philosophers we will be considering!)

Plato idolized Socrates. He attended the trial that condemned his teacher to death, and was 31 when Socrates was executed in 399 BC. It is generally accepted that Plato's early works represent very closely the views of Socrates, as expressed in a series of dialogues. However, from this basis, Plato developed several quite specific and original streams of thought – none of which can be summarized properly in an outline of this length. His less well-known thinking on brands and branding, however, lies at the heart of much that follows in this slim volume. As with much of his more mainstream philosophy, his thinking in this area was one of the single biggest influences on the philosophy of branding. To understand the role it played, we need to understand something of Plato's doctrine of Forms or Ideas.

Worlds apart

Plato could see that, in a world of flux where things come into being, change and pass away, everything is transient. To this extent he was in agreement with Heraclitus. But Plato took this train of thought one big step further. Everything we see and experience around us, he therefore said, can only be an ephemeral representation of a more real and permanent world that exists outside time and space. Behind the apparent disorder of this world, exists a highly ordered reality – not perceivable through our senses, but approachable through our minds.

This means that *total* reality is in fact divided into two: the changing bit – the world of flux – which we experience through our senses, and the *un*changing bit which we cannot experience, but only glimpse through our mental reflections (or perhaps through 'religious' experience).

The implications of this approach are clearly far-reaching – not least in the way it suggests that the *true* nature of everything is invisible to us. All of which means that the world which we *can* and *do* experience is no more than a superficial sequence of changes through time and space – a world that is summed up in the phrase 'everything is becoming, nothing is'. This was the jumping-off point for Plato's work on branding.

In creating for the first time in effect a sophisticated definition of what a brand is, he built on Heraclitus's position, and made it clear that a brand *as we experience it* should never be seen as something that is, but rather as something that is always *becoming*.

Working at two levels

At one level this may seem quite obvious – but it is key both to the way brands 'work', and to the way brand marketers should approach their task. In other words, the real challenge of brand management at the broadest level is always to manage a brand in terms of what it can *become* (for people), rather than to manage it in terms of what it *is*. Or, to put it another way, brand management is about the (future) ways in which a brand can be experienced by its target consumers. A brand is not simply an entity to be preserved.

However (and this is a big 'however'), in trying to manage the process of becoming, it is important at every stage to relate the brand back to those elements of it which are, or should be, unchanging. And this is key – for herein lies one of the most fundamental thoughts about the management of brands: the critical relationship between the ever-changing ('becoming') ephemeral side of the brand, and the largely unchanging things which underpin its whole *raison d'être*.

A brand is therefore something that exists for us at two levels. At the visible, tangible level it is a part of our everyday reality. But at a deeper, invisible (and, to some extent, ultimately untouchable) level, it is rooted in something unchanging.

Let's try to explain this more by tracing it back to Plato's main point about the world of Forms – the world which underpins the superficial world that we experience. The Form of something is what gives it permanence and point. Here's an example. There are many different chairs in the world of experience: they are all different – they serve different purposes, in different places, and no one of them is more a chair than any other. In the world of Forms, however, there exists 'chair' in a purer sense: a Form that stands behind, as it were, every chair that we could possibly experience in the world of ephemera – a superficial world which, in itself, cannot be trusted to show us 'the truth'.

For this reason Plato did not like the arts. The arts create beautiful representations in the world of ephemera that appeal to the senses, but which have no equivalent in the world of Forms. That, said Plato, was sheer indulgence, and could not possibly help towards an appreciation of the way things are in reality. For the same sorts of reasons, he warned about creating 'brands' that exist for people only at a surface level – the level of immediate consumer experience. What he urged was the need for brands that are rooted in those fundamentals that constitute true reality.

The myth of the brand

Many readers may have heard of Plato's 'Myth of the Cave' – probably the most well-known part of the *Republic*. Far fewer people, however, know of his 'Myth of the Brand'. I therefore set it out here in a shortened form.

Imagine, Plato said, a large, dark room in an ancient Athenian house. Facing one wall on a row of chairs sit a group of ten consumers. They have been told that they must focus their gaze only on the wall in front of them; they are not allowed to turn round.

At the back of the room a large fiery torch is lit. It casts light all around, and in particular onto the wall at which the consumers are gazing. Between the torch and the row of consumers are placed in turn various well-known Ancient Greek objects: an earthenware pot, a pair of sandals, a comb. Each object can be defined both in terms of its function (we know what it *is*), and its particular 'branded' style (eg the handles of the pot are distinctive, the sandals have a unique form of strapping, the comb a characteristic shape).

The objects throw shadows onto the wall in front of the audience, and the consumers are able to recognize the various brands on this basis. This early 'magic lantern show' is the equivalent of a modern-day presentation of brand logos, pack designs, or advertising executions.

The point being made is quite simple. The audience may be able to recognize one object from another, even one *brand* from another, on the basis of what is projected onto the wall – but what is being experienced is far less than 'reality'.

Plato is saying that, in the same way that the shadows on the wall are a limited and superficial projection of the different objects, so too are brands *as we most immediately experience them* a superficial projection of something more 'real'.

Representation and reality

To summarize, then – Plato saw brands working at two levels: the brand as experienced by the consumer at a superficial level, and the brand that 'stands behind' what is on the surface.

His point was that the first, more immediate level is always *becoming*, and therefore is, and must be, subject to change on an ongoing basis. The second level, however, represents a more permanent and unchanging reality for the brand. In some senses, therefore, he brought together the key branding points that had been raised by Heraclitus and by Socrates – the points about flux and about pinning down values.

Plato's great step forward in terms of brand management was that he clearly saw the relationship between the two, and the way in which both are vitally important for the health of a brand over time.

This is something we need to remind ourselves of constantly in the way we seek to manage brands today. Sometimes, our modern, apparently sophisticated approaches to brand management blur the distinction that Plato was trying to make. We talk about brands having functional attributes, emotional attributes, values, personalities, and so on – but we often lose sight of the fundamental split that ensures that successful brands must be *at the same time* both 'of the moment' *and* 'enduring'.

It is therefore quite salutary to remind ourselves of the split Plato introduced – whether we call it Body and Soul, or Representation and Reality, or something else. First, what constitutes the brand, how is it experienced by consumers in the here and now, and what is it in the process of becoming? And then what is its 'Soul'? What stands behind its current projection as something that has *meaning over time*, and that constitutes the basis for a deeper relationship with consumers?

This duality, and various builds on it, lie at the heart of much of the whole philosophy of branding. It is therefore perhaps easy to see why some people have seen the history of that philosophy as, in some respects, footnotes on the ideas of Plato.

Plato's top tip

Your brand should have two natures. At one level, its superficial nature should always be in the process of becoming (something else) – otherwise it will not be 'of the moment'. At a deeper level, it will need to have values that do not change over time, and which 'stand behind' the superficial characteristics of the brand.

4 Aristotle – and the importance of structure

So far, so good. Heraclitus, Socrates, Plato – it all seems to be heading in the same direction.

One of the most engaging things about philosophy of any kind, however, is that philosophers tend not to agree with one another. In fact, much of the point of philosophy is derived from the way one view is brought into sharp relief by another view (sometimes leading to the emergence of yet another – third – view).

It's something worth bearing in mind as we come to consider Aristotle's philosophy of branding in relation to Plato's. Aristotle was Plato's pupil – which means that, quite incredibly, the three greatest Greek philosophers were all linked by personal contact. He was born in 384 BC, and died aged 62 in 322 BC.

The biggest point over which Aristotle took issue with Plato was the latter's insistence that reality consists of two worlds or dimensions – the world of the here and now (known through the senses), and that of ultimate truth (known through the intellect). This disagreement led Aristotle to a completely different view of what constituted the 'essence' of a brand. But we're getting ahead of ourselves. Let's first trace the key elements in Aristotle's thinking overall.

Aristotle was very clear in saying that we lose the plot if we allow ourselves to start talking about an intangible world that lies beyond our personal experience. Only nonsense, he claimed, will be produced by basing a world view on something that we cannot know with any certainty. Quite sensible, you may say. And Aristotle was, in several senses, a very sensible man. (And, lest that seem a slightly damning description, it should be added that Aristotle has one of the foremost claims to being the most intelligent man that the Western world has ever produced.)

A 'scientific' approach

This point, however, about what can be *known*

establishes a fundamental difference with Plato. Indeed, it is a difference that characterizes the whole of the rest of Western philosophy. In effect it dramatized for the first time the split between those who see 'reality' as being beyond direct human experience, and those who see the only ground for philosophy as the world as we can see, hear, smell, and feel it. It's a split that we shall come up against again – and one that was only resolved (or largely so) by the work of Immanuel Kant some two thousand years later.

Aristotle was driven by an enormous hunger to understand the world of experience. Much of his life was therefore spent analysing and labelling the world in all its many diverse modes of being and spheres of activity. His own work and words virtually invented new fields of 'scientific' enquiry – fields like logic, political science, metaphysics and ethics. And he created words that we use every day in the world of branding – words like attribute, essence, property, category and proposition.

When Aristotle brought all this knowledge and insight to bear on the subject of brands and branding, his focus was therefore very clear. It was to look at brands in the real world (the only world) of experience – and to ask 'What is it for a brand to exist at all?'

He could, for example, look at a well-known style of

bread and recognize that, as a brand, it was more than just the sum of its ingredients. But *what* was it exactly?

He rejected Plato's view that a brand was determined largely by something in the world of Forms – a 'soul' which could be considered to be on a different plane to the here-and-now superficial nature of what was (staying with the bread example) on sale at the baker's.

But if the bread was anything more than the material of which it consisted, what exactly was it?

Structure and form

Let's leave the bread for a moment, and try to explain his approach by going back to the example used in the chapter on Heraclitus – the example of a BMW. A BMW (any BMW), said Aristotle, is made up of lots of bits. The bits in themselves, however, do not define a BMW. Most of the bits could be replaced by a different make (eg the tyres) or by a different material (the wheels) – and yet the finished article would still be a BMW.

Being a BMW, therefore, does not depend on the exact physical properties of the things that make it. What defines a BMW is its structure and its form.

What defines a brand, therefore, may well be more

than its constituent parts – but there is no need, said Aristotle, to appeal to matters of 'soul' or other worlds to make the point. A brand is a brand by virtue of its *form* – not the other-worldly 'Form' that Plato introduced into the equation, but rather the form that defines what something is – and is *for* – in this world.

Form is therefore what makes the thing a brand. Many of the bits that go to make up a BMW could be put together in a different 'form' to make a Saab or a Mercedes. If we were asked to describe a BMW (compared to, say, a Mercedes) we would probably start talking about matters of form – like the styling, the characteristic setting of the headlamps, etc. It's unlikely that we would first describe a BMW in terms of its engineering – even though we might know that the engineering was something key to the BMW brand.

This, in a nutshell, is Aristotle's point. He sees the form of the car as what constitutes the heart of the brand – and this is a good reminder to us that, in branding, we always need to keep our feet on the ground. It's all very well relating the brand to a set of *values* – but Aristotle reminds us that, if we lose sight of what a brand is *for*, we are indeed lost.

It was this idea that led Aristotle to define what he called his Four Causes of Branding – the four key things which he felt defined a brand.

The four causes of branding

The first cause he called the Material Cause. What is the brand *physically*? What is it made of? If it's a service rather than a product, how do you 'touch' it?

The second is the Efficient Cause – who makes the product or service, or who brings it to you? In most cases, this will simply be the name of the brand (BMW, IBM) – although in some cases it will be the name of the 'parent' brand, endorser, or house-brand (eg Apple for MacIntosh, Sony for Walkman).

Third is the Formal Cause. What gives the brand the shape by which you know it, and by which it is identified by the world at large?

And last but not least, the Final Cause – which is the ultimate reason for being. In most cases this will be the end benefit of the brand.

Through this approach Aristotle was attempting to escape the imprecision of Plato's duality, and pin brands down as things that could be precisely defined and developed. Brands are, he said, first and foremost real things that deliver benefits – and the moment we forget that is the moment we lose sight of reality.

Let's look at a couple of examples of the Four Causes and how they define brands in Aristotle's terms.

The Material Cause of Diet Coke is that it is a carbonated drink. The Efficient Cause is that it is brought to you by Coca-Cola – a universally known brand with a wealth of heritage. The Formal Cause is the characteristic pack design that I'm sure every reader would readily identify. And the Final Cause is something like 'Cool refreshment with no sugar'.

Or take the Walkman. The Material Cause is that it is portable hi-fi. The Efficient Cause is that it comes from Sony. The Formal Cause is how it looks: we all know what a Walkman looks like. And the Final Cause would be 'state-of-the-art music on the move' – or words to that effect.

In these examples, I've added some subjective 'values' into the Final Cause – but, in some respects, this is an indulgence. The fact is that the approach works just as well with a more utilitarian or functional proposition. And, in some respects, this was Aristotle's point – that the true essence of a brand is not a set of values or something subjective, but rather something that is manifested in its *function*. If you describe a brand in terms of what it is, where it's from, what it looks like, and what it delivers (ie what it's *for*), then – to all intents and purposes – you have left nothing unsaid.

A brand is what it does

When it comes down to it, a brand is what it *does*. Consumers never ask what a brand is: that question is only ever asked by brand marketers. Real consumers are only concerned with one thing: what is a brand *for*? Any approach to branding that forgets that, and substitutes instead a philosophy based on brand values, is doomed to failure.

At one level, of course, we all know this. Think of the brands that have tried to extend into categories and markets outside their core. In most cases, the failures (and there are many of them) were not because the *values* were not transferable. They probably were. It was rather that the brand was unable to persuade a (largely sensible) public that it had any real reason (or right) to be in that new market in the first place.

Aristotle it was, therefore, who (in a sense) first warned about all those well-intentioned, but ultimately pointless, stretches that prove that (with a few exceptions in the fashion industry) the brands that last over time are those that offer a sustainable product or service benefit. They are not simply nice bundles of touchy-feely values.

Aristotle gave us, for the first time, a sense of design

and *structure* in the way we approach brands and branding. As we shall see, the history of the philosophy of branding in more modern times was largely a working out of the challenges that had been thrown down by the Ancient Greeks – at the centre of which was the challenge and the need to balance Plato's intangible values with Aristotle's functional benefits.

Aristotle's top tip

Always ask what the brand is *for* – and what does it 'do' that makes it demonstrably better than others in the same market or category? Unless there is a clear functional reason for buying the brand, the consumer will soon fall out of love with it. And remember that you need to ask this question of the brand in all its manifestations – especially when stretches are being considered that take it outside its core market or category.

PART II

I think, therefore I brand

We now jump forward nearly 2,000 years, and pick up the thread around the year 1600. Does this mean that there was no Western philosophy – and no philosophy of branding – for all that time?

Not at all. But it *is* fair to say that no single philosopher was in quite the same mould as Plato and Aristotle until Descartes arrived on the scene. Two main reasons contributed to this: the so-called 'Dark Ages' and the rise of Christianity.

While the Dark Ages were not nearly as dark as we're often led to believe, they were not conducive to either 'pure' philosophical thought or to branding. The key intellectual and cultural focus for the Western world during the period between the end of the Roman empire and the Renaissance was Christianity. This meant that many of the greatest thinkers of the time were what we might call 'career Christians' – most notably Augustine of Hippo (AD 354–430) and Thomas Aquinas (1225–74).

By the 17th century a dramatic change had set in. The writers of the 17th and 18th centuries were still at least nominally Christian – but their enquiries were now clearly focused on establishing a new basis of knowledge in a more 'worldly' context. This provided a base from which the philosophy of branding could be taken forward in a number of key areas:

- the first 'scientific' view of branding, based on a rational approach to consumer understanding;
- the need to take a holistic view of the brand, and to validate assumptions about it;
- the establishment of *experience* as a counter to the rational approach;
- the recognition of feelings and emotions as the drivers of consumer choice.

5 Descartes – and the application of Reason

René Descartes gave history one of its most famous quotations: *Cogito ergo sum*, which is usually translated as 'I think, therefore I am'. Less well known is his ungrammatical *Cogito ergo significans sum* ('I think, therefore I make known by brands').

Needless to say, Descartes' contribution to philosophy generally – and to the philosophy of branding in particular – went a lot further than a couple of phrases.

He was born in France in 1596, and as a young man quickly displayed his brilliance as a thinker in law, mathematics and philosophy. The central question that dominated his life as a thinker was this: can we know anything for certain?

This obsession was driven by his work as a mathematician. It was in this field that his genius first flourished. (He invented analytic, or coordinate, geometry – and also the graph.) Mathematics is closely related to philosophy in many respects, and several great philosophers have also been eminent mathematicians. At one level, mathematics shares with philosophy some common thought processes (like logic, for example). At another level, mathematics holds out a challenge to philosophy.

Mathematics is a conceptual science: it follows clear principles, is internally consistent as a 'system', and can also be validated by experience. Above all, it provides the best basis we have for *certainty*: if X, then Y (eg the square on the hippopotamus, and so on).

From Descartes' time until now, the single biggest challenge facing philosophy has been the extent to which it can 'copy' mathematics in providing a similar certainty. This was the quest that drove Descartes – and his philosophy is an expression of his desire to reach as scientific a level of knowledge as possible.

Let's see how he worked it out in the context of branding.

If X, then Y

Descartes knew that mathematics was rooted in a small number of clear and simple premises that could not be doubted. From that solid base, a chain of knowledge could be constructed link by link: if X, then Y; if Y, then Z; and so on. As mathematicians across the ages have found, the more links you add, the more you open up the possibility for new channels of investigation. The important things, however, are that (i) the approach is based on irreducible premises, and that (ii) the process of building on that base is completely transparent and open to scrutiny.

This philosophical method he saw as the basis for a more 'scientific' approach to brand management. What, he wondered, was the equivalent of an irreducible premise or starting point in the world of branding?

It was certainly not something 'out there', in the 'market', as far as he was concerned. This was not simply because he shared Heraclitus's view that everything was in flux. It was also because he had learnt not to trust what his senses told him. Something as simple as an optical illusion was enough to prove that we cannot trust our eyes – and the same could be said for *all* the ways in which we experience the world.

In the face of this, the only thing we can be certain of is what is going on inside our heads – what we *think*.

Descartes thought that the world existed at two levels: there is matter (what is 'out there'), and there is thought (what our minds are able to think). Because matter can deceive us, it is less reliable than what we can think.

Brands are thoughts

OK. This all sounds a bit heavy and theoretical. How did he apply it to branding? He had two main points.

First, brands exist only in the mind. We may talk about them in terms of their structures and designs, but those physical manifestations are just 'products'. Brands, as such, are different. They exist only as thoughts.

The red tin of fizzy drink on that table over there, and the thoughts I have in my head about Coca-Cola are different and separate. The Coke brand can be equated with the thoughts in my head more than it can with the tin of fizzy drink.

Second – and this was the big step forward – *all* thoughts are essentially brands or at least the basis for brands. Now this *does* need thinking about!

What he was saying was that, simply by thinking, we

create a world of meaning – and that our thoughts can be built up in logical and rational ways to create intelligible worlds full of intelligible brands. I think, therefore I think brands.

Now this may sound highly conceptual, but it's key. Let's reduce it to the simplest formula we can.

If brands are essentially thoughts, then all thoughts are potentially brands. The way to understand brands best is to reduce them to their core thoughts, and then work out from there.

This means that the fundamental need is to get inside people's heads in the first place. That's the only possible starting point for brand development and brand management. Otherwise there is no basis for anything.

In several ways, Descartes was creating the first sophisticated view of consumer research. He was saying that anything relating to a brand's material, efficient, formal or final causes (to use Aristotle's words for category, brand name, product design, and purpose/benefit) can only be approached through an understanding of what is going on in the consumer's mind at the deepest level.

Asking the question 'Why?'

Years ago, when I was working as a brand consultant, the marketing team of a leading retail bank announced at a meeting that they were about to launch a new automatic cash dispenser. When I asked what consumers thought about it, they looked at me blankly. They hadn't asked: the team was operating in a market where (certainly at that time) consumers got what they were given.

Now clearly the idea of consumer research wasn't invented by Descartes. People had been asking their customers for years what they thought about this or that. No one, however, had come up with the idea that the whole of branding actually starts with an understanding of what's going on in the consumer's head. It is only on this basis that a meaningful brand proposition and its various expressions can be built up in a rational way – if X, then Y; and if Y, then Z; and so on – but with everything being traceable back to some original 'certainties'.

In more recent years, this has been the process adopted through research techniques like 'laddering'. Here's an example of how questions are used to track back to the irreducible point that is the branding equivalent of 'I think, therefore I am':

Why do you drink Coke?

Because I like it more than other soft drinks.

Why?

Because it tastes like it's always tasted since I was a kid.

Why's that important?

Because I've got used to it.

Why's that important?

Because it gives me something I can rely on, and that doesn't change from one day to the next.

Why's that important?

Because I need some fixed points of reference in my life.

Why?

Because otherwise I wouldn't know who I was.

And so on.

Clearly this is a made-up and superficial example. But it demonstrates the power of the 'Why' question in reducing motivations back to their core. In this particular case, it makes the point that the core of the Coke brand is not its taste, but the fact that (for this fictitious consumer at least) it helps to tell me who I am.

At a simplistic level, … I think (identity), therefore I drink Coke.

Cartesian dualism

Now, as already suggested, what this does in branding terms is create two worlds. Not the two worlds of Plato – the world of enduring ideas and values and the world of transient expressions or 'shadows' – but rather two worlds where what is in the consumer's mind is different, and basically (so Descartes would say) more *certain*, from the world we see and touch.

We call this Cartesian dualism – 'Cartesian' being the adjective from Descartes. (Why not 'Descartesian', I wonder?)

What Descartes did was raise the importance of rationalism and logical deduction in the process of branding – and, above all, establish the importance of starting as close as possible to the root of all knowledge – ie something deep inside the consumer's mind.

This approach also created something of a *science* of branding. Branding, by this measure, is not primarily about the management of expressions (logos, designs, advertising, etc). It is about what we can *know* – about consumers, about markets, about whatever it takes.

Now, as we shall see, this runs the risk of losing the spirit of branding as, in essence, an intuitive and creative exercise. Brand management often suffers by being in the hands of people who know a lot, but who lack a natural and instinctive empathy with their brands and consumers.

The impact, however, of Cartesian rationalism cannot be denied – and there is a lot to be said for trying to establish a core of certainty around what consumers really, *really* think, and not allowing branding strategies to be led by whim or fashion. If it (whatever it is) cannot be proved, said Descartes, then it must be doubted.

As we shall see, rationalism of this kind is not the answer to everything – but Descartes' approach asked questions which every subsequent brand philosopher had to address.

Descartes' top tip

Do not relax until you have identified the irreducible ('certain') core of a brand – what drives its connection with consumers. This will mean getting inside consumers' heads, and understanding deep-seated motivations and thought processes. Once that is clear, the development of the brand mix should be a rational and logical working out from the core.

6 Spinoza and Leibniz – and a systematic approach

Lumping Spinoza and Leibniz together in the context of branding makes sense. But they were very different characters, with distinctly different philosophies.

In 1632, when Descartes was approaching his most productive time as a philosopher, Baruch Spinoza was born in Amsterdam of Portuguese Jewish extraction. Twenty-four years later, Baruch left the Amsterdam Jewish community, changed his first name to Benedict, and set himself up as a grinder and polisher of spectacle lenses. This new, but solitary, profession enabled him to earn a living while he worked on his philosophical writings. From then until his death in 1677, he eschewed the offers of academic and public office which his writings brought him. Shortly after his death, his most famous book, simply called *Ethics*, was published. (The book is wide-ranging – certainly wider than ethics, as we would currently define that word.)

Comment has already been made (at the beginning of Chapter 4) about how philosophers tend to disagree with one another. Not surprisingly, in many cases the disagreement is with the views of the prevailing guru of the time. This was certainly the case with Spinoza. He began his philosophizing in a world that was beginning to be shaped by the new 'scientific' ideas of Descartes and Cartesian dualism (see Chapter 5).

Spinoza had a big problem with this. Where, he asked, in a world that works (and is understood) in terms of mathematical principles and certainties, is there room for 'God'? (We'll see in a minute why God appears here in inverted commas.)

Enter God

The only way Spinoza could see to get round this problem was to deny the fundamentals of Descartes' philosophy. Most importantly, he denied the distinction between matter and mind – between what is 'out there', and what we are able to think. To explain this we have to bring in God.

Descartes was working and writing very much in a Christian culture and tradition. Whatever he may have *thought*, to propound anything less than religious orthodoxy was not an option. ('I think, therefore I am a Christian' was pretty much taken for granted.) Descartes therefore invested time in 'proving' that God exists as an infinite and perfect being.

Spinoza took a big step on from here – a step which tried to stop Cartesian dualism in its tracks. He said that, OK, if God is infinite, then there can be nothing that is not God. Everything – yes, *everything* – must be part of the same one infiniteness. So, there can be no dualism – and no separation between 'God' and the world. They are the same. (Hence the inverted commas around 'God'.) One person may describe 'everything' in terms of a materialistic view of the universe (eg a collection of galaxies and solar systems). Another may describe it in a more religious, philosophical or abstract way. But, according to Spinoza, both are talking about exactly the same (one) thing.

This also applies to us as people. We are not bodies that have separate 'souls' (as suggested by Cartesian dualism). Each one of us is an entity: 'body' and 'soul' are simply two ways of talking about the same one person. The same thought drove Spinoza's philosophy of branding.

Two ways of saying the same thing

Spinoza liked some things about Descartes' approach to branding. In particular he liked Descartes' logical method for brand development. What he *didn't* like was the idea that what the consumer *thinks* about the brand, and what the brand is in *tangible* terms, are distinct and separate. He saw them simply as different ways of saying the same thing – and that, importantly, any brand should therefore be developed and managed as one integrated entity.

In support of this, he pointed towards the service sector. Given what we said in the last chapter about a certain retail bank, let's use that as our example here. With a bank there will always be specific 'product' elements of the service (like the functionality of its cash dispensers). For most of the time, however, what we *think* about the bank will be determined by its overall 'service' (helpfulness of staff, general facilities, speed of response/delivery, etc).

These things cannot be separated. The consumer's thoughts and the product/service are simply two ways of talking about the same experience. So, for example, the bank's innovation and communication are one and the same, and should be managed as such. In other words, the bank should not install new cash dispensers regardless of consumer research, while at the same time running an advertising campaign saying 'We listen'!

Leibniz did not consciously build on this, but his work helped suggest a way for marketers to avoid the risk of self-delusion (ie there's a difference between 'We listen' and 'We like to think we listen').

Defining truth

Gottfried Wilhelm Leibniz was born in Leipzig in 1646. He was the son of a philosophy professor, and at the age of 21 turned down the chance to be a professor himself. Leibniz's reasons for shunning the academic world were, however, different from Spinoza's. Far from wanting to hide himself away, Leibniz wanted to be active in the world of affairs.

Through his published writings, travelling and various positions as diplomat and courtier, he became a noted public figure. Behind the scenes, however, this gifted polymath was creating significant new concepts and systems of thought in a number of areas. For example, he was a mathematician of genius, inventing calculus independently of Newton. (It is Leibniz's 'system' that has prevailed.)

When it came to the philosophy of branding, his biggest contribution was in the way he formalized the definition of truth.

He defined two logical types of truth in terms of two kinds of statements. The first kind of statement is true (or false) within its own terms. The second kind of statement is only true or false depending on 'facts' *outside* the statement, ie the statement is not self-sufficient.

An example: 'Smoking does not damage your health.' This statement is false because it is clearly self-contradictory. We know (well, most of us do) that smoking *does* damage your health. We may nevertheless choose to smoke – that's another matter – but we cannot claim that by doing so we are not damaging ourselves. The evidence is so clear that the statement above is similar to saying that 'The sun is not hot.'

But what about *this* statement? 'Alcohol in moderation is beneficial.' Is this true or false? The answer is that we cannot tell from the statement alone. What does 'in moderation' mean? Or 'beneficial'? And beneficial for whom? It cannot be declared true or false without further enquiry and more 'facts'.

Analytic and synthetic statements

In the first example, the truth can be established by analysing the statement. This kind of statement therefore became known as an *analytic* statement. In the second example, the statement requires us to consider additional inputs. Philosophy refers to this as a *synthetic* statement.

What Leibniz's work does is force a distinction between these two different kinds of truth with a view to avoiding the trap of self-delusion – a constant threat if brand managers become blinded by their own vision of how things might be.

Let's look at a brand like Disney. What are some of the 'truths' about Disney that we (as its brand manager) might want to claim?

- Disney's business is family entertainment.
- Disney provides escapism.
- Disney's primary channels are films and videos.
- Disney offers friendly service.

And so on.

Now, how many of these are analytic statements and how many are synthetic? Well, interpretations may differ, but broadly speaking we can say that 'Disney's business is family entertainment' is analytic, in the same way that 'A conjuror performs magic tricks' is analytic.

On the other hand, 'Disney offers friendly service' is synthetic, in the same way that 'Everyone enjoys a conjuror's tricks' is synthetic. It is a statement that requires validation by other 'facts'.

OK. Admittedly this is a very simplified, black and white example – but Leibniz's point was clear. When you talk about your brand it's very easy to lump together statements which are unquestionably 'true', and statements which you'd *like* to be true.

How does this play to what Spinoza was saying? Spinoza wanted to make clear that a brand as a tangible product or service, and my *thoughts* about that brand are simply two ways of talking about the same thing. The brand's development should not be managed, therefore, as a series of separate processes (eg an innovation strategy focused on one thing, and a communication strategy focused on something else).

Putting that into practice is then helped by Leibniz's distinction. We need to be clear whether what we are saying about the brand really is a 'truth', or whether it is simply something that we as brand managers would like to believe. (In talking about brand image, for example, marketers can often muddle their 'vision' with what is the current reality as consumers understand it.)

In short, if a statement about the brand is not analytic, then it must be subject to ongoing validation.

Spinoza's and Leibniz's top tips

From Spinoza, the development of a brand's tangible properties and how consumers *think* about the brand overall should not be managed as if they were separate. So make sure, for example, that your innovation and communication strategies are clearly in sync.

Leibniz then prompts us to make a distinction between what is incontrovertibly true about a brand, and what we would *like* people to think about it. Any statement about a brand that is *not* self-evident must be subject to ongoing validation as part of the process of moving it from current reality towards where we want it to be.

---

7 Locke – and the empirical tradition

John Locke's name is less well known than that of several other great Western philosophers – yet his contribution to the development of modern thinking (and to the philosophy of branding) is amongst the biggest of any we shall be considering.

Locke was born in the west of England in 1632 (the same year as Spinoza) and grew up during the turbulent times of the English Civil War, the Interregnum, the Restoration, and the so-called 'Glorious Revolution of 1688'. In 1689 he published his greatest work, something he had been developing for almost 20 years – his *Essay Concerning Human Understanding*.

The developments in England between 1650 and 1700 sowed the seeds for the future of democratic government, both in Britain and in the United States a century later. This formative period of history was characterized as much by radical thinking as it was by constitutional reform, and Locke played a prominent role in shaping its intellectual spirit.

He was very much part of the Parliamentarian movement during this time, and was in several senses a 'liberal' politician and writer. He died in 1704, at a time when political stability had largely been restored, and the beginnings of modern parliamentary democracy established.

A sensible man

John Locke was above all a sensible man and a sensible philosopher. This is meant as a compliment. He was sensible in several ways. First, he was never a slave to his own (or anyone else's) theories – particularly if they looked like leading him to the wrong conclusions. Second, his views were very much in step with much of what we now take for granted in the way we conduct and govern ourselves in a modern Western democratic society. So much so, in fact, that several of his arguments (in favour of toleration, for example) seem rather self-evident to us – although, at the time they were penned, they were far from being so.

Third, he put *sense* itself at the centre of the philosophical agenda – and nowhere more so than in the philosophy of branding. Let's focus then on that.

In a nutshell his view was that our *experience* of the world is the only reference point for how we progress. Reason, in terms of mental processes, cannot give us all the answers – and is the wrong place to start. A better test of reality is what our *senses* tell us. Indeed, it's impossible for us to perceive things in any way that is *not* sensory – and that should provide some guidelines for how we manage brands.

We need to trace this thinking through step by step – but it's important to note at this stage that what is being challenged is primarily the rational and logical approach that assumes that everything can be worked out on the basis of what we can *think*.

Locke starts by reminding us that everything of which we have any knowledge at all is experienced by us through our consciousness – and that, of course, includes our knowledge of brands. Our consciousness receives a variety of inputs – some intellectual, some emotional, some sensory, and so on. Locke calls all these inputs or data 'ideas'.

Constructing our consciousness

Our conscious minds he sees as, in effect, empty, white spaces or blank sheets of paper on which the ideas make their various marks. I experience a concept (eg if X, then Y), and it becomes part of my consciousness – a mark on the blank page. I feel sorrow, and that too leaves its mark. The same thing happens when I hear a sound, see a colour, or smell a smell. Any brand I encounter, therefore, I encounter via my senses before it ever becomes a 'thought' as such. If we continue to use our Coca-Cola example, I experience Coke as a number of different 'ideas': look, taste, smell, logo, advertising, etc.

All these inputs build up a store of references from which we can construct increasingly complex pictures of the way the world works, and the role of brands within that. Our memories act as ordering mechanisms that collect, store and then cross-reference the data – and, over time, we develop an ability to make sense of the different ideas as they relate to each other. In effect, we construct our consciousness on the basis of the various inputs we receive – in this case, *brand* ideas.

The important thing to grasp here is that our senses form the *only* interface between the world of brands and our ability to grasp and understand that world.

Even in the case of an intellectual concept ('if X, then Y' or 'The ultimate driving machine'), I can only know this idea by either hearing it or seeing it. The only channels for ideas are therefore the senses: ideas exist on the 'outside', and are transmitted to the 'inside' (of our heads) through our senses. Our heads then assemble the ideas into something that can be made sense of.

This thought process is what we refer to as *empiricism* – an approach that was to create a strong tradition in the philosophy of branding ('brand empiricism'), and one that was at variance with the approach of pure reason.

Brand empiricism

Brand empiricism is primarily different to Cartesian rationalism in that it dismisses the notion that there are thoughts rooted deep inside us, around which brands can be created and developed. According to brand empiricism, brand building is less about unlocking primal consumer motivations, and more about creating constructs of ideas that make sense (to consumers).

Brand empiricism therefore makes clear that everything we know, believe, and hold dear about a brand has been transmitted to us from 'outside'. If I, as a consumer, say that one brand is 'better' than another, it is because that thought has been built up in my mind (by direct or indirect experience of the brand), and not primarily because the brand resonates with a deep-seated need in me. *The brand, through its characteristics, has created and articulated the need – and not the other way around.*

What Locke does, therefore, is get us to focus on the way brands contribute to the build-up of sensory cues in our consciousness – and he does this by creating some distinctions. All brands, he says, have certain characteristics that are *objective* – that is, they are characteristics that do not depend on your or my personal perception of them. And because these characteristics are objective, they are measurable. For example, in the case of a product brand, its size, shape, weight, and so on. These Locke called the brand's 'primary qualities'.

There is then a second set of qualities based around the way a brand is related to each consumer – things that *cannot* be measured in a similarly objective way. This would include, for example, a brand's smell, feel, perceived benefit, etc. These Locke called the brand's 'secondary qualities'. This difference, between primary and secondary qualities, Locke felt was essential in understanding the true nature of a brand – and how to develop and manage it.

So, the primary qualities of Coca-Cola are those physical attributes of the drink and the packaging that can be measured, 'scientifically' verified and stated as objective 'facts'. The secondary qualities of Coke include its perceived benefits (eg refreshment, image), but also (interestingly) its colour and taste – since these cannot be stated as objective 'facts': they are dependent on interactions with each consumer's subjective experience. Their management, therefore, is a less precise 'science'.

A case of induction

OK so far? Right, now it starts getting a bit more complicated. Two points. First, because we can only know a brand through the way its characteristics make an impression on our consciousness, we can therefore not know it *in itself.* What we perceive is simply our sense impressions of something that must forever remain beyond our direct experience. (So let's not kid ourselves that we can ever get closer than those sense impressions. The brand does not have some independent 'life' somewhere.)

Second, Descartes said you can build a brand by

starting with what consumers think at the deepest level, and then working out from there through a series of logical steps. His approach was based on *deduction*: you start with a primal thought or premise, and then build the brand by applying that thought to the world of experience.

Locke said the opposite. A brand is only built by adding together a whole range of sensory perceptions. There is no mathematical model that says 'if X, then Y'. In fact, adding together sensory perceptions almost certainly means that mistakes will be made – and sometimes you will have to go back to square one and add them up differently. This approach is based on *induction*: you start with the world as it is, and then work back to the brand opportunity.

This was the key difference in the empirical tradition – and it forms a strong thread that runs right through the philosophy of branding from Heraclitus to Popper. The thought is simply that, as things change in the world of experience, brands need to change their premises or reasons-to-be – otherwise they will quickly find themselves out of step with reality.

Locke's top tip

By all means hold fast to a brand's characteristics – but don't lose sight of the fact that those characteristics are what we as brand developers create through its primary and secondary qualities. They are there to be managed, and need above all to be in tune with the way the world is now.

8 Hume – and the limits of Reason

In many respects, Hume represents the high-water mark of the British empirical tradition. Certainly there was no comparable UK-based philosopher of distinction until Bertrand Russell, more than a hundred and fifty years later.

David Hume was born in 1711, seven years after the death of Locke. He therefore grew up in a very different social and political culture, even though he shared several of his predecessor's main premises. Most of his life was spent in France and his native Edinburgh. By the time of his death in 1776, he had earned an international reputation as an essayist, historian and economist (Adam Smith was a close friend), but remained largely unknown as a philosopher. The publication of his masterly *A Treatise on Human Nature* in 1739–40 (when he was only 28) went unnoticed, as did several of his subsequent philosophical works.

That was to change three years after his death with the publication of his *Dialogues concerning Natural Religion*. From then on his reputation as one of the most direct, rigorous and original of all Western philosophers was firmly established.

To understand his particular views on branding we need to start by understanding the role he played within the empirical tradition that was effectively 'kicked off' by John Locke.

All about perception

Hume was in no doubt that all our apparent knowledge comes via experience – either directly to us as individuals, or indirectly via the experience of others. Knowledge is therefore the word we use to describe what we *perceive*: it is subjective, and cannot be regarded as offering any objective 'proof' that things are at all as they appear. Our lives are based, at best, around probabilities, and not certainties – of which more anon.

The same applies to the development and management of brands. For all that Reason would like to suggest that branding follows logical principles and is therefore something of a 'science', it is in fact nothing of the kind. The only way to approach brands is by treating them as clusters of individual sensations and experiences that may or may not be consistent or predictable – or even related to each other.

Any brand is a package of these disparate consumer experiences. It is the combination of how the brand is seen and understood by everyone who buys it, uses it, or influences the way it is perceived by others. No brand is any one piece of its mix (eg its advertising), at any one place or time. And it is certainly not what is written down in the brand manager's positioning statement, or in the brand mission statement.

OK, you say, this is pretty much the course that Locke was steering: the brand as a highly subjective entity, based on sensory cues of one kind or another. So what's Hume saying that's different?

To answer that, we need to raise the spectre of *causality*.

The conundrum of causality

What do you remember of Chapter 1, on Heraclitus?

Do you remember the bit about not being able to step in the same river twice? And that you will not be developing the same brand in the same market two days running? Yes, I know we agreed that, at one level, it's an absurd thought – and that, of course, we have to make *some* assumptions about the way the world works from day to day, otherwise we wouldn't be able to do *anything*.

Just as we have to assume that the sun will rise tomorrow.

But do we have any 'proof' that it *will* rise? Well, Hume very clearly said 'No'. And to understand why he said what he said about branding, we need to touch briefly on how he approached *causality*.

Causality is a real conundrum – and so this next bit may strike you as a touch counter-intuitive! At one level, it looks fairly obvious. At another level, it is deeply complex – and basically something that still has not been 'solved' from a philosophical point of view. OK – where do we start?

If the world – and the world of brands – exists for us as a bundle of individual sensations and experiences, is there any evidence for those things being linked at all by causality? In other words, *proof* that one thing causes another (if X, then Y). Hume's simple answer was 'No'.

You have a headache. You take some ibuprofen. The headache disappears. Great. Did the drug do the business? Almost certainly, you say. But you cannot *prove* that relationship. You are unable to claim it as a certainty because there is no clear evidence of a causal relationship. Your headache may have disappeared for other reasons – and, even though we can prove the medical effects of the drug on your physiognomy, it is impossible to prove that it was *this* that removed the feeling of pain you were experiencing. All we can say with certainty is that one thing (the disappearance of your headache) *followed* another thing (taking the ibuprofen).

In the same way, we cannot say with certainty that the sun will rise tomorrow.

The best argument in the world – probably

But hang on, you say, … it's risen every morning for … well, forever! Why should tomorrow be any different?

Indeed. But past performance does not provide a rational, logical basis for future activity. (Ask any stockbroker!) One day (day?) the sun will *not* rise – probably.

And that's the key. *Probably.*

We make our world intelligible – and liveable in – by working on the basis of probability, not certainty.

Certainty exists only in the rarified arena of mathematics: elsewhere it is a chimera. As we shall see in a later chapter, the world of science may sometimes like to *think* that it is built on a rock-like and rational foundation, but it is as un-certain as the rest of life.

Now you may consider all this an affront to your common sense. But read on. Because Hume moves us away from the causality cul-de-sac into a wide road of positive thinking for brands and brand management.

The argument goes something like this – and starts from our earlier, simpler empirical model. Brands are experiences and sensations. We cannot manage them rationally any more than we can manage *any*thing rationally. To base any of our branding strategies on Reason is to build our house on sand. BUT ... (and here's the 'build' as they say) ... BUT that is no cause for concern, because it is not Reason that drives our lives – and those of our consumers – anyway.

I do not eat lunch because, having considered the evidence for eating or not eating, I come to the rational conclusion that eating will be better for my well-being. I eat lunch because I am hungry, or because it breaks up the day, or because I have *always* eaten lunch (and observe that most other people in privileged Western societies do so too).

The same is true of the way brands work. Consumers choose and consume brands out of desire, or instinct, or habit, or whatever. They do *not* choose and consume brands because they have put themselves through a rational process of thinking.

Relegating the role of Reason

The key to the management of brands and branding, says Hume, is feelings, emotions, and passions – rather than thoughts. Reason has a role, but it is a secondary role – a role to order, sort and adapt our feelings.

Hume's great breakthrough was in pointing out that the choices we make as consumers are based on connections that we perceive, but which we are unable to prove. Connections that we *feel* are 'right', rather than *know* to be right.

An example. Look at L'Oréal's impressive range of haircare and skincare products. Many of the products or sub-brands base their propositions on having 'ingredient X' or 'factor Y' as the basis for delivering a particular benefit. Now, the rationalist would assume that consumers choose the brand because they are persuaded by the logic and the supporting evidence. But Hume knew this wasn't the case. He knew that the rational understanding was there to reinforce a *feeling* that consumers had about the brand, and not the other way round.

This opened wide the whole debate about the nature

of brands and branding. Putting together the various threads of Hume's thinking, it led to one conclusion: we cannot really know anything with certainty. We may have expectations (that the sun will rise tomorrow) and experiences (it rose today) – but they do not add up to real knowledge.

We must therefore remain open all the time to the possibility that we may be wrong – about anything. Or about everything.

But that in itself doesn't mean we have to be nervous about the way we develop and manage brands. Quite the opposite, in fact.

Because nothing is certain, we should be always experimenting – worrying less about whether what we are doing fits our theoretical models, and more about whether or not it plays to our consumers' feelings, emotions and passions. They (the brand's consumers) will not have arranged those feelings in a necessarily rational or predictable way – and neither should we manage our brands along those lines either.

Hume's top tip

Don't be constrained by an overly rational or logical approach to what you are doing. Reason has its limits – and it's not what drives consumer choice. Much better to focus on people's feelings and emotions. Above all, don't be a slave to your own theories about brands and branding!

PART III

Into the deep

David Hume and Jean-Jacques Rousseau shared the same world – but in some respects a gulf separates the traditions they represent. The difference is not unrelated to geography. By Hume's day, Great Britain had embarked on a course of development that had already been largely determined in terms of its purpose, structure and institutions. Continental Europe, on the other hand, was about to undergo half a century at least of revolutionary upheaval.

The increasingly nationalistic Europe for which Hegel and Nietzsche were (to some extent unwittingly) preparing their manifestos was a world away from the late Renaissance culture that shaped Descartes.

At the centre of the turbulence sat Kant, calmly and methodically piecing together the basis for a comprehensive philosophy that, once conceived, could not be undone.

It was a time when the philosophy of branding was taken into deeper and more difficult waters than at any time up to that point. Between the end of the 17th century and the end of the 18th century, the thinking that would influence brands and branding advanced on four main fronts:

- Emotion and feeling were put at the heart of the philosophical agenda as an alternative to a wholly rationalist approach.
- The worlds of 'Brand Empiricism' and pure Reason were brought together in a new way that suggested for the first time the real limits of branding knowledge.
- The idea of a branding *process* was established at the centre of brand management.
- The creation and primacy of brand values were advocated in a completely new and challenging way.

9 Rousseau – and the importance of feeling

While there is clearly some continuity between David Hume and Jean-Jacques Rousseau (especially as regards an emphasis on *feeling*), their differences represent something of a dramatic shift in the way Western civilization was moving.

The two men were almost exact contemporaries. They knew each other, and respected each other's work – at least until Rousseau's paranoia got the better of him. Indeed, Rousseau's sojourn in England during the mid-1760s was at Hume's suggestion.

And yet, for all that they were both products of the

same age, Rousseau has subsequently been seen less as a mid-18th century *philosophe* and man of letters, and more as the totem of an altogether more 'Romantic' and revolutionary movement. Why was this the case – and how did it exhibit itself in his philosophy of branding?

Rousseau was born in Geneva in 1712. Geneva was a sovereign state at that time, and the independence it represented coloured the way Rousseau saw himself in relation to culture and 'authority'. For all that he spent much of his life in France, for example, he never considered himself as French, or as part of a French literary or philosophical tradition. His upbringing was disjointed and emotionally fraught – certainly on the evidence of his extraordinary *Confessions*, which were published after his death in 1778.

The *Confessions* make for compelling reading – and there are undoubtedly some aspects of Rousseau that make him a sympathetic character. He is in so many ways representative of the human condition – strung out somewhere between hope and despair. But, to approach the creativity of his thinking, one has first to see beyond the desperately insecure individual who increasingly saw threats and plots around every corner.

The Social Contract and *Emile*

Against our more modern ideas of psycho-analysis, it is perhaps not surprising that a gifted individual boasting a turbulent childhood, tortured soul, incontinent constitution and tendency to paranoia should have produced such a flow of original thought.

Two literary works stand out above the rest in terms of the impact they have had – and both were completed within a year of each other. *The Social Contract* begins with the famous words 'Man was born free, and everywhere he is in chains'. This slim volume develops the concept of the 'general will' of the people – an idea that was to be core to much of the thinking of the French revolutionaries of the 1790s (and that also, one might argue, sowed some of the seeds of 20th-century totalitarianism).

The other book was *Emile* – in effect, the first attempt to deal with education as a developmental process which should be led by 'Nature' rather than nurture. (It is still required reading on many teacher training courses.)

What influence did these two works, and the rest of Rousseau's output, have on the philosophy of branding?

Three thoughts in particular drive the approach:

1. a rational way of looking at life is positively wrong;
2. the 'answer' lies in Nature; and
3. the 'general will' is more powerful, and beneficial, than individual wills.

Let's look at each in turn.

The primacy of nature

First, Rousseau turned on its head the notion that Western civilization – in its state of 'Enlightenment', based on a largely rational way of looking at the world – was necessarily a 'good thing'.

For Rousseau, it was positively a bad thing to be led by Reason. The appeal to Reason suppressed a more natural way in which we should approach the whole of life – including branding. He was therefore against the way in which branding had developed largely as a rational science, focused around ideas of 'managing' the thought processes of consumers.

Second – and building on the first point – he insisted that Reason should not simply be balanced by a recognition of our dependence on sensations (part of

Hume's message), but should rather be overthrown as the reference point for the way the world works. In place of Reason, he put forward 'Nature' as the answer – by which he largely meant instinct and feeling.

That this had implications for the world of branding was clear. Less clear, however, was what it should mean in practice. How, asked the brand marketers of the day, can brands be developed and managed over time if we jettison a rationally based approach to marketing?

It may well be appropriate to temper or augment Reason, they said, but is not rationalism in *some* shape or form indispensable? How else can brands and branding be managed in a rigorous, robust and sustainable way?

Fair enough, you might say. But Rousseau was unrelenting. The routines and rhythms of Reason, he insisted, are just so many psychological constraints that we have built to hide from ourselves the true nature of branding. Reason shields from us the otherwise glaringly obvious admission that brands are appeals to the heart, and not to the head.

He thus put at the centre of branding for the first time *emotional* values – almost to the exclusion of everything else. Brands must be powerful expressions of people's *feelings*, because only that will ensure that they really meet deeply felt needs.

Emotional values

This leads to a clear diminution of a brand's functional attributes – and so is a dramatic revision to a tradition that went back to the Ancient Greeks. Aristotle had suggested that brands must be talked about in terms of what they are *for* – by which he meant primarily their *function*. For Rousseau, what a brand is for is defined entirely in terms of *emotion*.

Choosing a brand is therefore much more about aligning with a set of values than it is about buying a set of attributes. This in itself is not new (think of our BMW example in Chapter 1) – but the Rousseau-esque approach opens it up to wider opportunities (and some risks as well).

Both are in the realm of brand stretch. Opportunities first. If your brand stands for 'Nature' (or 'Status' or 'Cool' or 'Fun', etc), then your range of products and services can be anything that enables consumers to align themselves with the values of 'Nature' (or whatever). We see this most obviously in the way designer names are applied to everything lifestyle, from clothes to fragrances to accessories (like spectacles, jewellery, etc).

The risks are also clear, however, and were warned about as early as Aristotle. They are mostly about forgetting the core of the brand in terms of product/delivery (its original reason-to-be), and then taking it into categories where it has no particular competence (let alone competitive edge). We've already alluded to the familiar mistakes that get made through overstretching.

The point behind Rousseau's emphasis on feelings also plays a role in the third point: that relating to the 'general will'. While Rousseau's overall approach was about glorifying emotion, his formulation of the general will was in several respects coldly logical. In essence, this is how it worked in terms of *The Social Contract.*

The best interests of society as a whole will not be served by a collection of individual wills – most of which will be pulling in different directions. Much better that everyone should sign up behind a 'general will' which will deliver recognized benefits for the entire society, even if that means that, in some cases, it is at variance with individual wills (ie personal freedom). Once the general will has been ascertained, it should be single-mindedly adhered to (ie enforced). Hence my earlier reference to the seeds of totalitarianism.

Aligning with big feelings

Applying this to the philosophy of branding does not, however, simply lead to a definition of corporate power, eg 'you choose what we allow you to choose, not what you really want'.

The Rousseau insight – especially linked to his emphasis on feelings and emotions – takes us closer to something else, which is about people's desire to align with big, emotional expressions.

The approach to thinking – and democracy – that was led by John Locke put the emphasis on toleration and freedom of choice. This was for a number of reasons – not least of which was Locke's view that no one political model was ever likely to be 100 per cent right when seen in the light of real human experience.

Applied to branding, the Lockean approach leads to what today we call micro-marketing, where every consumer is an individual – and there is no 'one size fits all'. It's very tempting to think that, in a complex multi-channel world, this is the *only* way in which branding can evolve.

Rousseau would have disagreed. Once we come at branding from the point of view of feelings and emotions, rather than Reason, we will come to a different conclusion – which is borne out by our experience of the way people align themselves.

People *like* to associate with other people in sharing the big feelings, important values and strong emotions of life. (Look at the way mass celebration or mass mourning seems to have a momentum all of its own.)

There is something about the 'general will', therefore, in terms of *feelings*, which is an important consideration for brand marketers of all kinds – and it was Rousseau who put that emotionally charged view of life at the centre of the branding debate.

Rousseau's top tip

Reason is not the answer. Branding is about feelings and emotions. It is about our 'Nature' as human beings. The power of branding comes from being able to step away from the constraints of Reason. Trust your instinct and your heart – and don't underestimate the power of aligning people behind big emotional values.

10 Kant – and a balanced approach

Several of the philosophers referred to in this book have been discussed in terms of their greatness, or the importance of the impact they made on Western thinking. If it came to a question of who was *the* greatest, however, there would almost certainly be two main contenders. One would be Plato (see Chapter 3). The other would be Kant.

That's the first thing to be said about Kant. That he was the dog's bollocks in terms of philosophers.

The second thing to say about Kant, however, is to warn you about rushing off to read him in the original (or, at least, an English translation of the original German). Unless you are going to dedicate yourself to understanding Kant in some depth, don't do it. His writings – with a few exceptions (of which more anon) – constitute some of the most impenetrable stuff I have ever stuck my nose in. Almost all of the little I know about Kant is at second or third hand – but, for most of us, that's the best place to start. (For example, in several respects Kant is best understood through the writings of Schopenhauer.)

OK. So much for the health warning. Now, why is Kant so important? And, more specifically, why is he important for the philosophy of branding?

The crux of the matter is that he brought together in a compelling way the two major strands of thinking that have been winding themselves through this little book since Chapter 5. That is Reason on the one hand, and Empiricism on the other. What can be *thought* (as it were, from 'inside'), and what can be *experienced* (as it were, from 'outside').

Moreover, he did this in a way that (really for the first time) put a clear limit on what we are able to know (and what we are *not* able to know). Although several aspects of his thinking have been 'improved' and developed by subsequent thinkers, no one has really managed to argue away the 'full stop' that Kant inserted into the Western philosophical tradition. For example, Kant effectively killed the debate around 'metaphysics', and made it clear that the existence of God simply cannot be proved (or disproved, for that matter).

Let's take a brief look at the man himself, and then try to trace some of his key thoughts as they were expressed through his philosophy of branding.

A methodical man

His dates are 1724–1804 – so he lived a long life that encompassed, but stretched beyond, those of Hume and Rousseau. That life was spent entirely in the provincial East Prussian town of Königsberg, where he was born, became a professor of philosophy, and died.

Although a quiet and methodical man, his brilliance as an original thinker was always in evidence. Interestingly, however, it was only at the age of 57 that he published the book that was to establish his reputation for all time. His *Critique of Pure Reason*, published in 1781, is one of the most important philosophical works of all time. Kant followed it with two more major works – the *Critique of Practical Reason* in 1788, and the *Critique of Judgement* in 1790.

The reception of the *Critique of Pure Reason* was not overwhelming. In fact, it was very much the opposite. (It's not only *me* that has found Kant difficult!) So two years later he published a much shorter work with a much longer title: *Prolegemena To Any Future Metaphysics That Will Be Able To Come Forward As Science.*

Prolegemena (as the book is snappily known – and which means 'introductory observations') basically summarizes the key points from the *Critique of Pure Reason* in a much more accessible style.

So, what does it all boil down to – specifically in terms of branding? It all comes down to what we are able to *know.*

When Kant was alive, the common view was that there was no limit to what we can know about consumers, markets, brands and branding. This is also a widely held belief today amongst those who see marketing as a 'science'.

The view goes something like this. We can either *think* our way through to 'the answer', or we can work it out from *experience* – but, one way or another, we'll get there in the end. We can find out whatever there is to be found out. We can talk to consumers, look at trends, develop new methods, and basically increase our knowledge of brands and branding until we know everything there is to know.

The brand marketer is therefore in the driving seat. So long as she or he continues to build up that knowledge base, consumer relevance and competitive advantage will follow as a matter of course.

We can only know what we can know

Kant begged to differ. He pointed out that our knowledge of consumers, markets and brands is not only determined by what there is to know. It is also determined by what *we are capable of knowing* – by the 'equipment' we have for understanding. By 'equipment' we mean at *least* our bodily senses and our mental faculties – and, by extension, our *tools* for gathering, assimilating and using knowledge (eg market research methods, idea generation techniques, etc).

In the same way that our eyes will not hear sounds – which can only be picked up by our ears – so too will our various approaches to consumers, markets and brands only give us readings on things they are set up to read.

'Indeed,' you may say. 'But isn't that obvious?' Well, *is* it? Let's look at an example.

My stated aim as a brand marketer may be to understand the underlying motivations that cause target group X to buy brand Z on an occasional basis. However, if my methods are focused less on underlying motivations, and more on top-of-the-head responses, and if I talk to a target group which is X + Y, rather than focusing only on X ... then, for all that I *think* I may have 'done the job', I will miss the mark.

And although this may well appear very simple and obvious, I have to say it happens all the time in brand management. Research is done. Decisions are made. Quite often there is no real connection between them.

All equipment does a *specific* job. Real life tends not to be characterized by too many Swiss Army knives, if you get my drift – single tools that allow you both to open tins *and* get things out of horses' hooves! The point is very simple. If your equipment is not designed to detect X, you will not know that X exists.

Radio waves are invisible to us. We know they're there because radio equipment tells us so. At one level, what Kant did was point out to brand marketers what they did *not* know – and perhaps *could* not know.

The limits of knowledge

Now this sets up an interesting new idea in the philosophy of branding. If what we can know about consumers and brands is limited, the sum of that knowledge must by definition be *less than the totality of the interplay between consumers and brands*. What we must be careful of, therefore, is assuming that what we can know is the *same* as the totality.

I must not assume, for example, that the Habits & Attitudes study I have just completed is anything other than a partial view of my consumers' habits and attitudes. Similarly, I must not assume that any Consumer Mind Tracking Study I conduct will in any sense give me a complete picture of 'the consumer's mind'.

What I have to do is remind myself of the difference between the representation of reality (what I can get hold of), and reality itself (which, in its fullness, I can never know).

Now, you may be thinking to yourself, what difference can this possibly make? If I can never know the fullness of reality, why should I worry about it? If the representation (be it a tracking study or whatever) is all that I can get hold of, then isn't that as firm a base for action as I'm ever likely to have?

Well, yes. Except that what this line of thinking does is prompt us to recognize that what we *take* to be reality is as dependent on what we are able to get hold of as it is on 'reality'. In other words, our understanding of consumers, markets and brands is determined more by a subjective view of the world than it is by an 'objective' one.

Frameworks within which we think

Think about it. Our understanding of consumers, markets and brands tends to be ordered and arranged in patterns. We create models and segmentations, hierarchies of 'need' and brand architectures. What Kant made clear is that this ordering is much more about the ways *our* minds work (as brand marketers) than it is about the way reality really is.

The connections we see in the world (in terms of time, space and causality) are the very things that make life 'manageable' – but those connections are based on thinking frameworks that are *in us*. They are determined by the subject (the observer) rather than being an inherent quality of the object (the observed).

In this respect Kant was taking a balanced view between the pure rationalists ('everything can be worked out in thought') and the brand empiricists ('our minds are blank sheets on which the things of experience draw their shape'). He was positing the idea that there is an important interaction between the two, and that our minds *order* the empirical world in very specific ways.

But he was also doing much more than just combining and balancing two different viewpoints. He was demonstrating very clearly for the first time ever that our understanding of brands and consumers as real experiences is dependent on mental models – and that it is these models that enable us to classify and categorize markets. The world is not arranged in 'objective' categories – and in brand marketing (if not in other areas of life) we can change the way consumers, markets and brands are categorized by *changing the way we think about them.*

Whether or not you think you already know this, it is probably the most potent idea that the modern brand marketer has in her or his armoury.

Kant's top tip

Don't be fooled into thinking you can know everything about your consumers, markets and brands. You will only see, hear, smell and feel what your 'equipment' allows you to. Are you setting things up to tell you what you want to know?

And remember that the 'categories' in which you perceive the world are much more to do with the models in your head than they are to do with 'reality' as such. Often the most powerful changes come about through changes in the perception of 'categories' (eg how you segment a market).

11 Hegel – and the primacy of process

Georg Wilhelm Friedrich Hegel was born in Stuttgart in 1770. He came relatively late to philosophy, but by the time of his death in 1831 he was recognized as the leading figure of German intellectual life. His reputation and influence continued to grow over the rest of the 19th century, as his ideas were picked up and developed by other prominent thinkers. Indeed, in practical and political terms, the full harvest of the Hegelian tradition appeared only in the 20th century.

So much for the cryptic introduction (which I'll try

to explain below). But how did all this relate to a philosophy of brands and branding?

One of the things that has probably become clear so far in this short book is the centrality of the idea of change and movement – and the attempts of various philosophers to understand how we perceive and experience the flux that is constantly going on around us.

We saw it in Chapter 1 when we looked at Heraclitus – and its influence has never been far from the areas under discussion. In essence, Hegel was the first philosopher to see this change in a wholly systematic way, and as part of a recognizable process.

Like Heraclitus all those years before, and like far more recent thinkers (for example, his contemporary, Friedrich Schelling, 1775–1854), Hegel saw reality as organic, inherently unstable, and constantly in a state of becoming something else.

History as a process

An important difference that Hegel (and Schelling) exhibited in comparison with many previous thinkers was the thought that this process of change had both an underlying structure and an ultimate end.

It was therefore not simply change for change sake.

There was something going on that was moving, consciously or not, towards a goal – with that goal being self-fulfilment and understanding. History was not simply a sequence of events. It was a process through which the world, and everyone in it, was moving towards completeness and self-realization.

This is what reality was. An historical process – and a process through which the essence of life itself was growing towards its ultimate state of utter harmony and self-knowledge. Hegel called this essence of life *Geist* – a word that is difficult to translate from the German, but which includes a sense of 'consciousness' as well as 'spirit'.

This is the basic idea that led to more than a century of cataclysmic intellectual and then political upheaval. It's an idea that spawned extreme ideo-logical traditions, both right-wing and left-wing. So how did that happen?

In terms of Hegel's *right*-wing followers, it began with a perceived association between the ideal state of utter harmony and the real state of Prussia during the early years of the 19th century. The philosophy added credence to a growing feeling of (what was to become) German nationalism – and a theme that can be traced through to Hitler.

The influence of Hegel on *left*-wing politics was due almost entirely to one man – Karl Marx. Marx took over wholesale the idea of reality as an historical process – although he saw its subject as materialistic, economic and political rather than as something concerned with *Geist*.

The intellectual father, therefore, of both Nazism and Communism – Hegel has a lot to answer for!

But how did his basic ideas get applied to brands and branding?

The dialectic

The starting point (and end point) for his philosophy of branding was this idea of *process*. Everything to do with brands and branding is the outcome of a process. Nothing is *not* the result of a process. Therefore we understand all that we understand in terms of a process. And, what is more, that process will always be capable of being understood.

Indeed, the process can always be described in the same terms – whether it is about changes in consumer behaviour, the emergence of a new market or the development of a brand over time.

The key is to recognize that all the varied and

complex situations that surround us as brand managers and marketers have within them areas of conflict and tension. It is because of this that the world appears (and indeed is) inherently unstable.

The only way to move on and reach something new and productive is to resolve the current conflicts and tensions. This is the essence of the challenge, therefore, for brands and branding: how to create new and positive opportunities by bringing together apparently opposing elements. I'll give a couple of examples below of how this approach can be used to create new and powerful brand propositions. But first we need to understand the stages of the process – a process that Hegel called the dialectical process (or just simply 'the dialectic' – a word we encountered earlier in the context of Socrates' questioning method).

The first stage is the *thesis*. This is the dominant state of affairs as it currently exists. The second stage is the *antithesis*. This is the reaction that has been provoked by the thesis. The conflict and tension between the thesis and the antithesis is then resolved through a third stage which we call the *synthesis*. The synthesis then becomes the dominant state of affairs, and so the whole thing starts again.

Getting to the next stage first

We can recognize this in many areas of marketing and branding history. Let's take just a couple of examples.

Butter was once the thing everyone (who could afford it) put on her or his bread. Then soft margarine came along as an alternative. It had less (good) taste, but offered other benefits – it was cheaper, and easier to spread straight from the fridge. The tension between these two then spawned various (literally 'synthetic') brands: cheaper 'butters', spreadable butters, margarines with (buttery) taste, and so on.

Or take cars. It's quite natural these days to think in terms of cars that offer both performance and space/safety. Go back 10 or more years, however, and it was much harder to find mainstream cars that were sold on anything other than a single main benefit or image. Part of the change has, of course, been driven by technology – but a lot of it has been driven by brand marketers moving through to a new synthesis.

Think of opportunities in your own market. Let's assume your brand is brand leader and that your proposition is 'black' (thesis). Almost certainly, you'll have a competitor whose proposition is 'white' (antithesis). Are you going to wait for someone else to come up with the synthesis – or are you going to get there first? And remember, the synthesis will not always be 'grey' (ie a compromise – neither one thing nor another). It might be black with white polka dots. Or a bold black and white check.

The fact is, as Hegel made very clear, things are not going to stay the same. That's the only thing you can be sure of. What he was proposing was the basis for a transparent process for *getting to the next stage*. That next stage will happen anyway – but Hegel's most dedicated and famous disciples did not simply *wait* for it to happen. They set out to make it happen more quickly (and, they hoped, more productively) than would have been the case otherwise.

Thus, although a description of Hegel's process sounds like a natural *evolution*, it has been applied in many cases to propel a *revolution*. And certainly, in terms of branding, the simple application of the dialectic to most markets can generate some quite revolutionary ideas. Go on – try colliding some conflicting and competitive attributes, values or benefits around your own brand, and see what you come up with. Some of the outcomes will be downright silly – but some could well be the next stage in your market's development.

Working with *the Zeitgeist*

However, just before you persuade yourself that the time is right for you to turn the marketplace on its head, please note a second (and related) big Hegelian idea.

If history is a process that follows certain patterns, then you cannot put yourself outside that historical process. The *Zeitgeist* (meaning quite literally 'the spirit of the time' – and different from the *Geist* mentioned earlier) will determine what you can and cannot do. So you can't, as it were, anticipate what your market will look like in 50 years' time – and, even if you could, you could not create an 'authentic' brand or product that had those characteristics in today's market. (For one thing, consumers would simply not be interested: they would regard it, if they regarded it at all, as an idea quite literally before its time – before its *Zeitgeist*.)

What you *can* do, though, is work at the leading edge of the *current Zeitgeist* – which is why so many innovations that are successful feel that they've arrived at just the right time. (And a lot of those that *don't* succeed feel like a bridge too far. In which case, try them again in a few years' time.)

Putting these two ideas together gives us a good

sense of the overall impact that Hegel's philosophy of branding has for us. For the first time in the history of Western thought Hegel insisted on seeing reality as an historical process – and that includes what we do as brand marketers. Which should remind us that everything we do can only really be understood in terms of how it came to be *in the first place,* what its relative position (versus the competition, etc) is *now,* and what it is in the process of *becoming.*

Hegel's top tip

Change is a process that can be understood, and fast-forwarded. Brand marketing is largely about getting to the next important 'synthesis' first. Instead of worrying about competitive tensions in the marketplace, therefore, set out to resolve them through new and creative combinations. You are more likely to be successful at this if you have a clear understanding of your brands and your markets within an historical, and process-driven, context.

12 Nietzsche – and the creation of values

Friedrich Nietzsche (1844–1900) takes our story up to the beginning of the 20th century. Along with a few Existentialists (whom we will look at in the next section), Nietzsche has been one of the most read, influential and 'popular' philosophers over the past 50 years. Much of the attraction is that he wrote not as a systematic philosopher (ie creating 'systems' of thought – like Kant or Hegel), but rather as a polemical essayist – using potent language in a stylish and uncompromising way to goad the reader into a re-evaluation of her or his values.

While it might be argued that no major philosopher was ever not clever, Nietzsche was a particularly brilliant scholar. He was a professor by his middle twenties, but then gave up the academic life to concentrate on his philosophical writings which culminated in what is today probably his most well-known title, *Thus Spake Zarathustra*, published in 1891.

Alas, that was really the beginning of the end. As his reputation grew over the following years, Nietzsche slipped further and further into madness – the result of tertiary syphilis. He remained incurably insane until he died in 1900 without ever becoming aware that he had in those last 10 years become internationally famous.

His philosophy of branding has been a powerful challenge to brand marketers ever since. Indeed, it could be argued that we will only see the real harvest of his thought in the years to come – as brand marketers strive to find ever more compelling drivers of competitive edge.

God is dead

Nietzsche's starting point was very clear. He saw the world as one entity – an entity that we experience directly in its totality. He therefore had no time for 'worlds' which are beyond our understanding. Neither did he have any time for 'God'. The expression 'God is dead' is his.

Far from leading him to a depressed and pessimistic world view, this way of thinking actually made him approach life very positively. If this life is everything there is, he argued, then we should live it to the full. This living life to the full, however, can only be done if we jettison those things that hold us back from achieving our potential – ie the outdated values that shackle us to a moribund belief in God and other worlds.

Values are key for Nietzsche – both to life overall and to branding in particular. He saw social values as having their origin in belief systems – but belief systems in which, nowadays, we quite literally have no faith. In particular, he saw our Western values as emanating from a mainly Christian cultural history – a movement which may well have shaped society as we know it, but in which the mass of people clearly no longer believe.

And in terms of branding specifically, he saw brands as being (in their own small way) simply another reflection of that wholly inappropriate and out-of-touch value system.

For Nietzsche the solution was obvious. Either we find a way of making existing values relevant to the current situation – or we invent new ones. New values would serve us better overall – and would also indicate what our brands need to be like if they are to provide us with real benefits.

Indeed, the argument can be taken further. Brands can, in fact, *lead* the creation of new values.

Hmmm ... so what does *that* mean exactly?

Towards a new set of values

OK, let's try this ... Our social values are, on the whole, based on trying to be nice to each other. Overt declarations of selfishness, for example, are considered to be anti-social. However, says Nietzsche, we only put a value on being nice to each other because we have grown used to two thousand years of wishy-washy Christian forbearance.

In a dog-eat-dog world – where most of us no longer make any pretence of being Christian – we would be much better off accepting that the key to survival and then success is in being stronger, more efficient, and more ruthless than the next woman (or man). Selfishness is not something to suppress, therefore – it is a value around which we could all (so the argument goes) cohere with a real sense of association.

Now, clearly, one cannot easily overturn two thousand years of cultural and moral history – except that, in *brands*, we have 'things' which have no real purpose other than to make themselves bigger, better and more successful by reflecting the values with which people want to associate.

Moreover, in trying to be distinctive and therefore competitive, brands will increasingly need to exemplify not the values that we *already* recognize and largely admire in our society, but rather the ones that we are less comfortable in owning up to (like selfishness).

The search for new values will become a necessity in branding – if only because *current* values are limited as a basis for new brand positionings. So Nietzsche's point can be expressed in the following terms: brands will need to stand for values that truly reflect the way we are, rather than the way we pretend to be, or assume ourselves to be. In so doing, brands and branding will therefore lead us towards a morality that is a more accurate reflection of our real beliefs and aspirations.

A prime target of this thinking is the apparent mediocrity of mass market branding – and, in that context, you can see that Nietzsche's approach can lead to the creation of niche brands. However, if he was right – and the 'new' values of such a niche brand are much closer to the way we really are – then the niche may eventually become something much, much bigger.

Working outside current constraints

Let's take a simple theoretical example based on the selfishness idea.

To proclaim selfishness overtly as a value would be seen in most quarters as mistaken or mischievous. However, to position a *brand* as selfish (or as something *for* selfish people) might be viewed with less obvious disapproval. And it would offer some consumers a way of admitting (at least to themselves) that they were indeed selfish: 'The brand exists. I'm simply buying it.'

What is more, by buying the brand, the consumer would – consciously or not – be joining together with a community of other selfish people. Brands are, after all, largely about communities of interest – ie values – and for a lot of the time, and for a lot of brands, what people are buying into is membership of one of these communities (or 'clubs').

Nietzsche's case underlying all this was coldly logical

– but still remains challenging, and somewhat counterintuitive, for minds that have been nurtured on apparently well-established moral systems. The point is this: if values are, indeed, human artefacts, then we can make and live by whatever values we like so long as they serve our interests.

The challenge this throws down to brand marketers is clear. It makes the whole *raison d'être* of branding the search for values which are seen to serve consumers' interests. And what Nietzsche is also making clear is that these interests are not simply the ones that consumers will tell us about. After all, people will in most cases play back the values with which they have been 'programmed'.

No, the 'secret' of branding that Nietzsche brought to the surface was that an understanding of *really* relevant values needs to look past what is socially acceptable, to reveal the way people might fulfil their potential if they were not operating within current 'moral' constraints.

That does not mean that brands should seek only to exemplify anti-social behaviour. New values will not always be as negative as selfishness. But there is certainly scope for brands to own more of the values that fall outside the 'safe' arenas of family, security, self-esteem and status. In the future we should expect to see more brands that declare themselves in terms of single-mindedness or opinionated-ness or wild imagination or conviction or abandonment. And so on.

A brand's will to power

In busy markets brands will only achieve distinctiveness by creating their own value systems – their own 'worlds' in which they can exemplify for consumers the ultimate expression of whatever that value is.

This quality in a brand is what Nietzsche calls its 'will to power'. Of humans who develop their potential fully in this respect he coined the term 'superman'. In the same way, brands that exhibit this same will to be almost quite literally a law unto themselves he called 'superbrands'. Superbrands are not simply great brands – they are brands which create their own worlds around them. In effect, they deny competition the ability to compete by defining the market as being the territory that the superbrand occupies.

At one level, this sounds like nonsense. Surely it is impossible to shut out competition? Astute competitors will simply redefine the market and the market rules.

Correct. But that is expensive – and in many cases it is an admission that the superbrand has indeed colonized a whole market around its values. Disney is a superbrand in this respect. You don't compete with Disney by being like Disney but better. You compete by being something else entirely. Microsoft is also a superbrand – and one that has even more obviously 'colonized' a market. (The 'market' is defined by what Microsoft does.)

Nietzsche's vision is one in which brands become organisms in their own right – expressions of values which, once set free, create their own momentum to fulfil what they have the capability to become.

It is certainly a world of brands and branding that is not for the faint-hearted!

Nietzsche's top tip

Values are at the heart of branding – but in a much more potent sense than we normally assume. Brand values should not just be 'attachments' to a product or service, but rather the driving force for what the brand can dare to become. Competitive edge lies in creating new values – perhaps risky values – rather than repackaging existing market values. The way to 'superbrands' is through owning the territory that goes with those values.

PART IV

Searching for certainty

The 20th century unravelled many of the certainties that Western civilization had become used to over the preceding five hundred years. The First World War redefined the scale and brutality of military conflict. The rise of Nazism and its consequences dealt a fatal blow to any notion that human consciousness and conduct was on an irreversible trend towards ever-greater enlightenment. People began to get used to a loss of structure and form – in the arts, in the institutions they had assumed to be 'for ever', and in their own domestic situations. And religion – once the lynchpin of social cohesion as much as an article of faith – increasingly dressed itself in the robes of irrelevance.

Western philosophy, like Christianity, largely chose the role of specialist commentator – and, in the face of monumental scientific and personal challenges, retreated from many of the biggest questions of the day. Instead, philosophy spent much of the 20th century debating with itself around the finer points of language.

There were, however, also some major contributions to the philosophy of branding – each of which reflected the increasingly challenging and busy world in which branding was called upon to play an ever-more prominent role.

- The critical move in thinking was away from the brand as a 'mark' that simply signified something, and towards an understanding of the brand as a tool for growth.
- In parallel with this came an appreciation that a brand is not simply something to be managed, but is also an individual entity that exists in its own right.
- Constructive criticism was brought to bear on

branding with a view to finding the next best model to drive growth.

- And the first moves were made to encourage the exploration of branding as a legitimate subject of philosophical enquiry.

13 Wittgenstein – and the brand as tool

Ludwig Wittgenstein was born in 1889 in Vienna, and died in 1951 – so he is the first of the philosophers we have considered who was very much a 20th-century figure. His adult life – lived largely in Britain – spanned the two world wars, and his legacy played a major part in forming the philosophical agenda of the second half of the century.

Wittgenstein came from a very wealthy industrial family, and arrived in England in 1908 to study aeronautical engineering at Manchester University. He soon became fascinated by the philosophical issues thrown up by higher-level mathematics – and this led him to leave his engineering studies and to take up philosophy at Cambridge under Bertrand Russell.

The philosophical tradition within which Wittgenstein formulated his own theories went back to Kant (and Schopenhauer). Like Kant, Wittgenstein saw the totality of the world as having two components: the bit that we perceive by virtue of our senses and are therefore able to talk about, and the bit we cannot perceive and are therefore unable to talk about in anything other than purely speculative terms.

For Wittgenstein, philosophy could only address the former – the bit we are able to talk about. To attempt to philosophize about the latter was, he asserted, a complete waste of time. It should therefore be a subject on which we remain silent.

From this starting point, Wittgenstein developed not one but *two* distinct philosophies – with the second one addressing what he considered to be the key flaws of the first.

The brand as picture

Wittgenstein's first major contribution to the philosophy of branding came in 1921 with the publication of

Tractatus Logico-Philosophicus. This set out to establish once and for all the limits of knowledge, ie what exactly it is that we are able to perceive and talk about. By the time he had finished the *Tractatus*, Wittgenstein felt he had emphatically put an end to the debate, and had clarified all the outstanding issues of philosophy. He did this by showing the connections between perception, thought, language and expression – with the biggest new element being around the centrality of language.

In broad terms the *Tractatus* set out its view of language in terms of what has been called Wittgenstein's 'picture theory of meaning'. As applied to brands and branding, the theory goes something like this.

One of the roles of brands is that they represent the world to us. They quite literally 'label' for us what might otherwise be an incredibly chaotic array of messages. Each brand does this job in basically the same way that a picture (a painting or a photograph) represents a particular part of the world to us.

A *picture* of a person or a thing is not the same as the person or thing itself. Nevertheless, the picture will contain (unless it is an abstract) the same elements as the person or thing it represents. It will, for example, present us with the same shapes and colours, and show them in the same relationship to each other in terms of space, size, and so on. Assuming that to be the case, we can recognize the picture as being a clear representation of the reality. We would not (in most cases) confuse the one for the other – but both picture and reality share common elements in the way they present themselves to our senses. Both picture and reality, argues Wittgenstein, share the same 'logical form'.

Logical form

The role of the brand is similar to that of the picture. What a brand does is to represent for us something that we value in the world at large. The brand in effect 'stands for' that something. To use a very simple example, Persil soap-powder in Britain in the 1960s was the 'logical form' of clean white clothes. Through the power and consistency of its communication, Persil 'stood for' whiteness.

Now clearly brands today still 'stand for' things – but in many respects the relationship between them and what it is they stand for is not quite as simple as a 'logical form'. This should not, however, deter us from regarding 'logical form' as a useful starting point in the development of brands today. The model represented by the picture theory of meaning still provides some potent lessons – even if those lessons cannot be applied in quite the same way that they could in the past.

If, for example, a brand can become *synonymous* with an important benefit (like Persil = whiteness), then it may well be able to maintain a dominant position for as long as that benefit is seen by consumers to be important. As brand marketers we talk nowadays about 'owning' a piece of territory in the mind of the consumer, and this is basically the same idea. The aim, if you like, of 'logical form' is to bring the brand and the thing it represents so close together that the brand in effect becomes the piece of language that consumers use to describe the thing.

As suggested, at one time this was relatively easy to see in the way brands worked. People would talk about real whiteness in terms of 'Persil whiteness'. (In some cases, the brand name even became the generic descriptor for the 'thing', as with Hoover or Biro – or, perhaps more recently, Post-It Notes.)

However, as also indicated, such 'ownership' becomes more and more difficult as markets become more congested and consumers become more sophisticated. Some would say that it is now almost impossible in mature (Western) markets. That's probably putting it too strongly – but it's certainly true that there are very few 'things' (emotional associations as well as functional features) that cannot be copied by other brands over time.

The demands of a complex world

But there is, of course, a *second* reason why Wittgenstein's picture theory of brand meaning has limitations. And that is driven by the need of brand marketers to make sure that their brands 'stand for' more than one thing.

In mature markets growth is usually dependent on moving into new sectors. Brands are therefore faced with a challenge that is fundamentally different from the one they faced 20 or 30 years ago. Today it is not enough for a brand to offer the logical form of one thing. In an increasing number of cases, a successful brand has to do two different (and potentially conflicting) things.

On the one hand it has to continue to 'stand for' something recognizable and valuable. On the other hand, that something has to be equally relevant *across* a number of sectors – within each of which the brand has *also* to prove its credentials on a sector-specific basis. For example, as the UK laundry market developed, Persil had to stand for things other than whiteness – both in terms of its over-reaching brand values, *and* in terms of the functional credentials that it could offer in particular sectors.

Wittgenstein could see this before it happened. He could see that the philosophy he had set out in the *Tractatus* was flawed: the picturing of an aspect of reality was only *one* of a brand's functions. Brands would need to do a great deal more than simply provide a one-for-one picture of something if they were to grow in an increasingly complex and complicated world.

He therefore set about creating a *second* philosophy of brands and branding – and one that would correct the limitations of the first.

The brand as tool

This second philosophy – also concerned with the same central issues of representation and language – only became fully clear after Wittgenstein's death through a range of posthumous writings, the most important of which was *Philosophical Investigations*, published in 1953.

In this second philosophical approach to branding, Wittgenstein moved away from the idea of a brand 'picturing' a thing. The new approach saw the brand not as a picture, but as a *tool*. The meaning of the brand was therefore not one thing – but rather a combination of *all* the things that could be done with such a tool. (If we stay with the simple laundry market example, it means that any leading detergent brand has to be able to 'fix' a *variety* of washing problems.)

This immediately suggests that the 'meaning' of a brand is unlikely to have one dimension only. Or, if it does have one dimension only, then that dimension has to be wide enough to encompass several 'things'. (Persil moved from 'whiteness' to 'care' as being the thing it *stood for*, whilst attempting at the same time to build functional credentials in a number of different but related sectors.)

At one level, therefore, the *meaning* of a brand is the combination of all the things it can stand for.

Clearly there is a fundamental shift here – and with that shift Wittgenstein's second (and ultimately more important) philosophy set the scene for many of today's branding dilemmas. The overriding challenge for most brand marketers today can be summed up in the balance that has to be achieved once you embrace the idea of the brand as tool.

The idea of the brand as tool means that brands are (or at least *can* be) whatever brand marketers want them to be. They are not (or should not) be limited by particular product attributes. They derive their meaning in the lives of consumers not from a simple surrogacy (Persil = whiteness), but rather from the many ways, and the many incarnations, in which they are understood and used every day.

Whilst the dangers inherent in this are clear (eg a potential licence for over-extension, loss of focus, etc), Wittgenstein's approach set the agenda – and the language – for much of our current debate around brand growth strategies.

Wittgenstein's top tip

Don't limit growth by thinking of a brand as 'standing for' one thing in the same way that a picture delineates a particular place or person. Think of your brand as a 'tool' that can, and should, have several uses and applications. A brand does not have only one 'meaning'. A brand's meaning is the combination of *all* its uses and values. The management of 'meaning' in this sense is the essence of modern brand management.

14 Existentialism – and the brand as individual

For the past 50 years, 'Existentialism' has been one of the first words learnt by aspiring young philosophy students. It is a word that (certainly for my generation) reeks of Parisian café society and a (by now) slightly dated and perhaps naïve thumbing of noses at the Establishment in all its guises.

For me, as a teenager growing up in the 1960s, it was a clear statement of intellectual fashion, with just enough of a whiff of revolution about it to make it slightly *risqué*. And yes, of course, it was predominantly French – and largely synonymous with Jean-Paul Sartre.

Now, none of this (as we shall see) is untrue – but it is only one part of what 'Existentialism' means. The fact that the word became a key part of the cultural consciousness of the last century is, of course, significant – but the origins and shape of Existentialism, particularly in the way it contributed to the philosophy of branding, have to be traced back much earlier than that.

The origins of Existentialism

Existentialism really began with Søren Kierkegaard, a Dane who was born in 1813 and died in 1855. The main thrust of Kierkegaard's thought was against what was then the prevailing Hegelian philosophical tradition (see Chapter 11 on Hegel).

Hegel's view was that everything can be explained in terms of all-encompassing movements, processes and systems. All individual developments are in some way connected as parts of a grand scheme that ultimately gives structure and purpose to the shape of history. Indeed, the fate of the individual cannot be understood outside this framework, and personal fulfilment can be attained only by submitting to and working with these relentless social surges.

Kierkegaard regarded this as nonsense. For him it was a fundamental error to suggest that existence could be analysed in terms of such sweeping movements, generalized trends and abstract concepts. If such broad conceptual approaches had any point at all it was to provide intellectual frameworks within which we might be able to see how things connected (spatially and temporally), and our role in relation to them.

But processes and systems – and even societies – do *not* exist as such, said Kierkegaard. Only individual entities exist. Those individual entities may choose – or be forced – to coalesce in particular ways, but that in itself did not militate against the idea that only individual entities truly exist.

The understanding of anything 'philosophical', therefore, must be based on an understanding of how and why individual entities exist. Hence, 'Existentialism'. The implications of this thinking for human beings are clear.

Hegel had said that individual human beings only fulfil themselves when they are subsumed in the greater whole and purpose of society. Against this Kierkegaard argued that the ultimate moral being is not society but the individual – and that therefore it is individual decision making that sets the measure for how human life is conducted. Existentialism is therefore largely about the way individuals give meaning to their lives through the decisions they make. (Parallels here can also be seen with Nietzsche, who urged the recreation of values to reflect 'real' motivations – see Chapter 12.)

So what does this means in terms of what we might call 'Brand Existentialism'?

Brand Existentialism

When applied to the philosophy of branding, the Existentialist approach provides a whole new marketing focus by looking at the opportunities in terms of the brand as a real and individual entity.

The main propagator of Existentialism in the 20th century was a German, Martin Heidegger (1889–1976). Born in the same year as Wittgenstein, Heidegger was a lifelong academic whose reputation suffered through his close association with the Nazis. His primary work on the subject, *Being and Time*, was published in 1927 – six years before the Nazis came to power – and is generally recognized to be the starting point for most 20th-century Brand Existentialism.

So what exactly *is* Brand Existentialism? In simple terms it is the dramatization of a brand's individualism or personality in a way that forces consumers to engage (or not) with it as part of their world.

That's how you recognize it. But what is it that drives such a marketing manifestation – philosophically speaking?

Brand Existentialism basically sets the brand up as an individual entity that is a real and integral part of the world in which we all live.

Brand Existentialism basically means that we cannot talk about a brand as if it were a concept or a label for something else (eg a set of values). A brand either is an individual entity in itself, or it is nothing. The key question to ask is therefore not (for example) what does this brand *stand for*, but rather what does it mean for this brand to exist at all? How do I recognize it – and experience it – as something that exists in the real world?

Now, you might argue that these questions can be answered simply by pointing to the brand in its most 'obvious' manifestations – the pack on the shelf, or the name over the door. Brand Existentialism, however, insists that the brand must assert its individuality and existence in a much more impactful and challenging way.

The question for brand marketers is then, 'So how do we make the brand exist for people in this more dramatic context?' The focus is less on giving a brand meaning, and more on giving it *life*.

Bringing the brand to life

Brand Existentialism insists that the most successful brands will be the ones that really do have a tangible existence in the world. Yes, brands need to 'stand for' the right sorts of things – but they also need to be active players in the lives of their consumers. The job of the brand marketer is therefore to make sure that the existence of the brand is brought to life in the strongest possible way.

The brand's essential existence is inseparable from having a world to exist in – and therefore one of the biggest tasks for the Brand Existentialist is to create a brand world in which the brand is the hero.

The term which comes closest to describing this in modern branding parlance is 'Experiential Marketing'.

The brand will only really have an existence when it takes up space and time in the world of consumers. This is not to say that brands should simply seek to make an impact through 'event marketing'. This will almost certainly be one important part of the total brand communication package, largely because 'events' offer opportunities for dramatizing the brand in new and unusual ways. The key, however, is in making sure that *whatever the brand does* is an authentic expression of its personality and purpose – in other words, its reason for existence.

This authenticity is critical. In a world of so many marketing messages – and in a world of apparently infinite potential segmentation – many brands will have to get used to the idea that whilst they may be 'must haves' for *some* people, for many others they may simply invite enmity. Such a polarization of views is not only inevitable – it also represents a coherent branding strategy for many brands.

And let's be clear – we're not talking about niche marketing here (ie a specialist offer). This is much more about the assertion of a brand's individualism – with all the implications (and risks) that such an assertion involves.

Giving a brand its freedom

It was this kind of thinking that was popularized in the

years immediately after the Second World War by Jean-Paul Sartre (1905–80). Sartre's most notable contribution to the philosophy of branding was the way he dramatized the *freedom* of the brand.

If a brand is *really* to have an existence that is more than just the sum of what people think about it, then that brand must choose or create its own values – and then live them. In effect, it must carve out for itself a space in the world and say 'Here I am. This is me. This is who I am, and what I stand for'. In this context, the core of the branding task is therefore about how a brand personality develops – and creates itself.

At one level, this may seem unexceptional. We all know that brands have values and personalities. How is this any different?

It's mainly different in the mindset that we, as brand marketers, bring to the development and management of the brand equity. Brand Existentialism demands that we allow our creation to be 'what it needs to be to fulfil its destiny'. Now, I've put those words in inverted commas because they look a bit – let's face it – plonky.

'Come on,' you might say. 'Brands are what we *manage*. They don't have any life other than the one we give them.' Well, yes – I know that. Which is why I started this bit by talking about mindset.

Brand Existentialism requires us at least to explore where a brand might go *if it were given charge of its own existence.* And, yes, I realize that this could turn out to be a bit like Frankenstein's monster! But it might also be a bit like allowing space for development and self-expression. (If you like, the brand marketer as an enlightened parent.)

One way or another, Brand Existentialism provides another useful pair of philosophical spectacles through which we can look for growth opportunities.

Existentialism's top tip

Avoid the temptation to be swept along by processes, systems, and 'the way we do it here'. Each brand is an individual entity that exists in its own right. If it *doesn't,* then it isn't really a brand in the full sense of being something with which people can have a relationship. So respect it as an individual, make bold decisions on its behalf – and create enough space for it to express itself in new, impactful (and sometimes surprising) ways.

15 Popper – and the quest for a better model

Before we can talk about Popper, we have to talk about Einstein. And before we can talk about Einstein, we have to talk about Newton.

Isaac Newton (1642—1727) was without doubt one of the greatest thinkers of all time. He was not a 'philosopher' as such: you *could* say that he was far more important than that! But it was his thinking that laid the foundations for much of our modern world and our understanding of 'science'. (Please note here the idea of Newton as a thinker.)

Now, it is no exaggeration to say that, during the two

hundred years that followed Newton's death, the Western world regarded his key discoveries as absolute certainties on the road towards a more complete knowledge of the universe. (Please note here the idea of Newton as a man who made 'discoveries'.)

Newton was seen to have *discovered* truths that, until then, had been hidden from the human mind. What he in fact did, however, was *think* his way through to a series of solutions to the problems he faced. Having thought of those solutions, he then validated them through mathematical calculations and experiments – and so demonstrated how they could be usefully applied in the practical world.

Now, what's the difference, you may say, between these two ways of describing Newton's phenomenal contribution to the advancement of our understanding? *Thinker* as opposed to *discoverer*?

The difference is that one approach – that of *discovery* – suggests the unveiling of hidden 'truths'. You can, as it were, only *discover* something that is 'there' (ie certain – or at least infinitely probable).

The other approach – that of *thinking* – is merely provisional (ie it is dependent on what can be thought).

Farewell to certain knowledge

You see, the mindset that saw Newton's ideas as *discoveries* assumed that what had been discovered constituted 'laws' – absolute laws which had quite literally been 'uncovered' by Newton's genius. If you like, a bit like an archaeologist brushing away the earth to reveal some hieroglyphic script – the secret language of how the world really is. After all, these laws 'worked', didn't they? You could apply them with confidence in all spheres of human endeavour.

What is more, this mindset assumed that you could continue to uncover more and more of these certainties through a cumulative process called *science* – and that gradually you would therefore be able to build up a comprehensive body of incontrovertible universal knowledge. Science was about the incremental addition (and connection) of these 'discoveries' – with the ultimate aim being a total comprehending of all that there was to understand.

Albert Einstein (1879–1955) turned that approach on its head. By in effect disproving Newtonian physics on several key points, Einstein demonstrated that what was previously assumed to be certain knowledge was something else entirely. In fact, Einstein dealt a severe blow to the entire concept of 'certain knowledge'.

What became clear for the first time was that Newton had not uncovered hidden certainty. What he had done was construct an intellectual model that 'worked'. It was not certain knowledge, but it 'did the job' – and to all intents and purposes constituted a full and predictive picture of reality.

Einstein replaced Newton's thinking framework (or at least part of it) with another, newer one more suited to 'doing the job' for our modern world.

There are few people nowadays who would suggest that Einstein's solutions constitute 'certain knowledge' any more than Newton's did – and, indeed, there is every reason to believe that yet another new intellectual framework will emerge as and when the current model is found to be wanting. (Witness the attempts at 'reconciling' Einsteinian physics and quantum mechanics, for example.)

The important thing – especially from the point of view of brands and branding – is this. *None* of these frameworks will be seen to have been 'knowledge' in the way that most scientists and philosophers before the 20th century thought about 'knowledge'.

But then perhaps all this is saying is that, for a long time, humanity has laboured under a misconception as to what 'knowledge' itself is. Perhaps knowledge is not certainty in any shape or form. It almost certainly (!)

cannot be equated with 'truth'. Perhaps 'knowledge' is simply what 'gets you through the night'.

Enter Popper.

Theory and practice

Karl Popper was born in Vienna in 1902, moved to New Zealand in 1937 to escape Nazi rule in Europe, and then in 1945 took up residence in Britain, where he stayed for the rest of his life. He died only in 1994, and so with Karl Popper our philosophy of branding comes pretty much up to date.

Popper picked up the challenges of scientific theory and knowledge, and applied them to the social and political arena – which includes, of course, the implications for brands and branding.

Popper started from the realization that scientific theories can never be 'proved' right. Two hundred years of successful working had clearly not 'proved' Newtonian physics to be 'right'. The fact that Newtonian physics 'worked' was not in itself proof of anything other than that the knowledge had a set of practical applications.

The only conclusion to be drawn from this was that *apparent* certainties were the products of human thought, and not 'objective facts'. And if this was true for 'science', then the same could be said of any sphere of human endeavour.

And so to branding … This short book has presented a range of intellectual theories and applied them to the world of brands and branding. Some of the theories were built on preceding theories – while others actively sought to overturn established ways of thinking. Some of the theories existed almost in a vacuum. The point is this. *None* of the approaches set out in this book – and none of the branding approaches set out in any *other* books you may have read – is anything other than someone's theory.

Some of those theories may be seen to 'work' better than others – but none of them constitutes any kind of certain knowledge about brands and branding. If we find theories that help us – and that seem to produce the right results – then we will go on using them until we find a better model. But we have to go forward in the full expectation that there *will be*, at some stage, a better model – and a better one after that.

New lamps for old

Our approach to brands and branding, therefore,

should be based above all on *a problem-solving mindset.* We must believe that we will move forward not by adding new certainties to our ever-growing bank of knowledge about brands and how they work – but that progress will come as we replace existing theories with new, and more productive, ones.

This should not be taken as a licence to change your mind every day about your brand vision and how to get there. But it should at least be an encouragement to look at new models, intellectual stimuli, practical examples and ways of thinking on a regular basis – if only to convince yourself that those new models and ways of thinking will *not* 'work' for your brand.

Not all the philosophical pointers and top tips of this book will necessarily help your brand to grow. Several of them, in any case, flatly contradict each other. But the point is that if you do not try a variety of thinking models, you will risk missing the next useful theoretical construct for moving your brand forward.

But how to do this?

Popper was clear. Although no theory can be proved right (in the way that two hundred years of Newtonian physics could not 'prove' Newton right), any theory can be *disproved.* Which is what Einstein did. This means that the chief method of the post-Einstein world is to seek to *disprove* alternative approaches to the way we might work as brand marketers.

What does this mean? It means, above all, fostering a culture of *criticism*. Constructive criticism – yes. But criticism nevertheless.

Continuous problem solving

The first major work in which Popper put forward these ideas was *The Logic of Scientific Discovery*, which was published in German in 1934, but in English only in 1959. This scientific approach was then developed in terms of its social and political implications, most notably in *The Open Society and its Enemies*, published in 1945. (By the way, unlike many of the philosophers we have been looking at, Popper's writing style is immensely clear and accessible – and *The Open Society* is a great read in its own right.)

Popper's argument throughout is that a single viewpoint is never justified, and that a healthier, more practical outcome will always be achieved through a pluralistic approach (ie more views, each based around the criticism of accepted positions).

This suggests that the most productive environment for brands and branding management is one that encourages openness and the constant criticizing of established views. Now, while this may hint at anarchy – or at least tend towards inefficiency (one of the drawbacks of most 'open societies'!) – it will almost certainly provide for an outcome based around a more workable and practical solution.

The desired mindset we should seek, therefore, is one of continuous problem solving – with the aim being less about building the perfect brand, and more about *removing the bits of the brand that do not work as well as they might.* This may suggest an incremental pragmatism at the expense of 'vision' – but it is likely to be a more realistic basis for long-term brand building.

In some respects, it is not a million miles away from what Socrates was suggesting almost 2,500 years ago (see Chapter 2).

Popper's top tip

Stop thinking in terms of certainties. They do not exist. You should always be looking to replace current ways of thinking with newer, better ones. Criticism is therefore where progress begins. The key is to see brand development in terms of continuous problem solving.

---

16 The future – and the real role of philosophy in branding

So, after all that, is there really any point in looking at brands and branding in terms of 'philosophy' – or has this whole treatise been an academic excursion with no practical use?

Well, not surprisingly, my view is that there *is* a role for philosophy in branding – and moreover, a role that goes further than the application of Socratic or Popperian wisdom.

There are two reasons for saying this.

First, brands and branding are fundamental to the

way we *experience* modern life – and the way we give 'meaning' to it.

Second, the primary role of the brand marketer is to *think* about her or his brand, and to create models for action that will motivate others (colleagues, customers and consumers).

Let's wrap up by taking a brief look at these two points.

The way we think

To suggest that brands are a fundamental part of modern life invites the riposte that this is only because giant corporations exploit the opportunities for managing consumer choice. That may well be an important issue for debate – but it is not the subject of this book.

If this book has any central point at all it is broader than the role of business in managing markets – although, clearly, one of the most immediate implications of the primacy of branding is the way consumer decisions are shaped.

The broader point is this: that brands and branding are features of the way the modern (Western) mind *thinks*. If I may exaggerate to make the point – it is impossible for the modern (Western) mind to think without recourse to the sorts of models we commonly refer to as brands.

What does this mean? In simple terms it means that most people spend most of their time thinking in terms of recognizable entities – be they products, personalities, services, television programmes, football teams, clubs, or whatever. This is not new, of course: we continually look for ways in which we can 'edit' the world around us. Today, however, it is far more pronounced than it has ever been in the past – simply because the number of *inputs* is growing at a frightening rate.

It's not simply that people are bombarded with more and more possible choices – although that is clearly the case for the majority of people in so-called sophisticated societies. It is also connected to the fact that most of the personal needs, wants and aspirations that we experience (or are at least able to articulate) already have their *solutions* somewhere 'out there'.

The territory of open-ended dreams ('I wish I could go to the moon') has been colonized by dream-package-providers ('Book now for space shuttle flights in 2010'). Life for many people is therefore characterized by a quest to find pre-packaged entities that match their wants, needs and aspirations.

Making connections

Now I'm no social scientist – so this may all be wrongheaded – but I think it's true that for a lot of people life is about the identification and assembly of these entities in a way that is more or less fulfilling.

And the biggest recent change in easily accessible technology supports this. The Internet is not simply a channel of almost infinite choice: its very mode of being suggests that you *will* be able to find the perfect match (for whatever it is you're seeking), just so long as you use the right search engine and type in the right words.

The result of all this is that our thinking processes are largely geared to making connections: to seeing the world as a place made up of defined entities – entities that are there and available for us to connect ourselves to. We seek to draw those entities, if you like, into some kind of association with our sense of who we are.

This is the world in which brands play. A brand is something that exists in a recognizable way – and that says 'you have found what you are looking for'. And the more that the world appears to us to work in this way, the more our thinking processes reflect that reality.

Within such a world we are able to use brands to *communicate* what we need, want and aspire towards. Brands not only constitute a *shorthand* for our wishes – they are also an articulation of desires which we would not (or perhaps *could* not) express otherwise. This is, of course, the root of the main criticism raised against brands as commercial tools – in that they *create* the desire, rather than simply satisfy it. Within this overall context, however, it is relatively easy to see how we can (and do) use brands to create *meaning* for ourselves and for others.

Now, lest this argument still brings to mind only images of soap powder, burger bars, and other 'packaged' goods and services, let's take a run at a couple of less obviously commercial examples – charities and churches.

Charities and churches

Charities have always faced the difficult job of getting people to part with their money. It's difficult not just because we're stingy, but also because people can find it difficult to discriminate between causes – and to feel any real connection with any one cause. (In some cases, that lack of connection is *precisely* what people want – 'Take my money – just don't tell me the gory details' – although that mindset does not usually constitute a sustainable revenue stream.)

This is where branding comes in – because a charity as a brand is not simply a 'cause', but also an association. The charity becomes one of the entities which reflects back on the individual's sense of who she or he is. At its most obvious (but also most potent) the charity can create the kind of association that few people will not want to be part of in some way or another (as with Comic Relief in the UK).

Ultimately the brand is about what I think and feel, and what *you* think and feel, rather than what the brand is in any objective sense. One of the strands of philosophy that runs through this book is that brands in themselves have no existence other than as they live in the hearts and minds of those whose action they are designed to motivate.

Now, if we look at churches we see a different way of relating brands to the thinking process. On the surface, churches ought to be very conscious of branding. In some respects, they *are* 'brands' already.

Christianity, for example, seen as a master-brand, has several sub-brands, one of which is the Church of England. The Church of England, being a broad church, has itself many sub-brands, eg Conservative Evangelical, Liberal Catholic, Traditional Catholic, and so on. And, of course, all these sub-brands have their own forms of 'packaging' (style of worship, of community, of building, of theology, of terminology, of ministerial dress, etc).

Why then are most non-churchgoers confused by what's 'on offer' at their local church (as opposed to the church half-a-mile down the road)?

It's largely, I would argue, because the Church of England has not woken up to the way that people think in terms of brands or entities with which they wish to form an association. Now please don't misunderstand me. I'm not talking here about 'marketing' as such: churches of all kinds already mount their own marketing campaigns – with mixed results. The point I'm trying to make is about the way people *think*.

If, as I'm suggesting, people think in terms of distinct entities presented in a relatively transparent way as a basis for choice and potential association, then the Church as a whole is missing the opportunity to connect with people at a fairly fundamental level. It's all very well to say that the 'message' (in the case of this example, the gospel) is its own commendation – but that is patently not the case. The fact is that by not addressing the way people *think*, the church will continue to disconnect itself from the vast majority of potential triallists.

The thinking brand manager

OK, so much for my first point – that brands and branding are fundamental to the way we *experience* modern life – and the way we give 'meaning' to it.

I'll be much shorter in covering the second point – which is to say that the primary role of the brand marketer is to *think* about her or his brand, and to *create models for action that will motivate others* (colleagues, customers and consumers).

This thought is prompted largely by seeing so many brand marketers over the years who treat their job as a series of brand management tasks without ever applying any real thinking to the whole point and meaning of it.

If brands and branding are as fundamental to the way we *all* think as I've suggested (and even if they're not!), then the primary job of a brand marketer must be to get one step ahead in her or his own thinking.

Now I know that the whole of this book runs the risk of appearing too cerebral in the face of very practical business challenges – like how to drive growth in an increasingly complex and crowded marketplace. But there is no escaping the fact that the best brands (by which I mean the brands that are most successful in their own terms) will be the ones that are driven and stewarded by people who can *think* their way to new, creative and viable opportunities.

This requires clever, intuitive, creative thinkers – and it needs an environment in which those people have the time and the space to think.

If brand marketers spend most of their work time 'managing' details that do not go to the heart of the brand, and very little time thinking about where the brand is going and how it connects to the way other people think – then none of us should be surprised if the brand hits the buffers. It may not be this year or next – but sure enough, it will.

Wrapping up

Right, that's enough preaching! I think the message is

clear by now. Philosophy has a role in branding – because branding is primarily about the way people *think*.

And, who knows, if there are any philosophers out there who agree with that suggestion, then perhaps branding will become a legitimate subject of philosophical enquiry.

But that's for the future. In setting out to write this book in the present, my primary target audience has been interested and open-minded marketers, rather than academics or philosophers. And in trying to get my message across I have, no doubt, mangled the thoughts and ideas of most of the great philosophers who feature in the book. For that I apologize.

The truth is, I am personally fascinated by philosophy every bit as much (probably more so) as I am by branding – and I hope that some of that enthusiasm will rub off on readers for whom the likes of Socrates and Wittgenstein may have been just names.

If you want to take your quest for thinking models to another level, there are a lot of good introductions to philosophy on the book shelves. I am personally indebted to Bryan Magee who, in my humble opinion, writes in a more accessible, engaging and knowledgeable way about philosophy than any one else I have come across. Any one of his several books surveying the Western world's philosophical tradition would be a good starting point for further enquiry.

But of course the point of this book is not to get you to run off in pursuit of the great philosophers, but rather to encourage the adoption of a quite literally more thoughtful approach to branding.

Let me end by directing readers to the Summary of Top Tips that follows on from this chapter. Those tips won't all apply, of course. But I'd be surprised if there wasn't at least one of them that would get you thinking in a whole new way about the branding opportunities that are there to be embraced in your own future.

Good luck!

Summary of top tips

Heraclitus's top tip

Assume that nothing is stable in the world in which your brand exists. Everything is always changing all the time. The relative position and perception of your brand will not be the same from one day to the next. It therefore has to be managed on the basis of constant flux.

Socrates' top tip

Question everything – literally everything – about your brand. Take nothing for granted. Always look to get to a deeper level of understanding. And don't settle for anything that doesn't feel like 'the truth'.

Plato's top tip

Your brand should have two natures. At one level, its superficial nature should always be in the process of becoming (something else) – otherwise it will not be 'of the moment'. At a deeper level, it will need to have values that do not change over time, and which 'stand behind' the superficial characteristics of the brand.

Aristotle's top tip

Always ask what the brand is *for* – and what does it 'do' that makes it demonstrably better than others in the same market or category? Unless there is a clear functional reason for buying the brand, the consumer will soon fall out of love with it. And remember that you need to ask this question of the brand in all its manifestations – especially when stretches are being considered that take it outside its core market or category.

Descartes' top tip

Do not relax until you have identified the irreducible ('certain') core of a brand – what drives its connection with consumers. This will mean getting inside consumers' heads, and understanding deep-seated motivations and thought processes. Once that is clear, the development of the brand mix should be a rational and logical working out from the core.

Spinoza's and Leibniz's top tips

From Spinoza, the development of a brand's tangible properties and how consumers *think* about the brand overall should not be managed as if they were separate. So make sure, for example, that your innovation and communication strategies are clearly in sync.

Leibniz then prompts us to make a distinction between what is incontrovertibly true about a brand, and what we would *like* people to think about it. Any statement about a brand that is *not* self-evident must be subject to ongoing validation as part of the process of moving it from current reality towards where we want it to be.

Locke's top tip

By all means hold fast to a brand's characteristics – but don't lose sight of the fact that those characteristics are what we as brand developers create through its primary and secondary qualities. They are there to be managed, and need above all to be in tune with the way the world is now.

Hume's top tip

Don't be constrained by an overly rational or logical approach to what you are doing. Reason has its limits – and it's not what drives consumer choice. Much better to focus on people's feelings and emotions. Above all, don't be a slave to your own theories about brands and branding!

Rousseau's top tip

Reason is not the answer. Branding is about feelings and emotions. It is about our 'Nature' as human beings. The power of branding comes from being able to step away from the constraints of Reason. Trust your instinct and your heart – and don't underestimate the power of aligning people behind big emotional values.

Kant's top tip

Don't be fooled into thinking you can know everything about your consumers, markets and brands. You will only see, hear, smell and feel what your 'equipment' allows you to. Are you setting things up to tell you what you want to know?

And remember that the 'categories' in which you perceive the world are much more to do with the models in your head than they are to do with 'reality' as such. Often the most powerful changes come about through changes in the perception of 'categories' (eg how you segment a market).

Hegel's top tip

Change is a process that can be understood, and fast-forwarded. Brand marketing is largely about getting to the next important 'synthesis' first. Instead of worrying about competitive tensions in the marketplace, therefore, set out to resolve them through new and creative combinations. You are more likely to be successful at this if you have a clear understanding of your brands and your markets within an historical, and process-driven, context.

Nietzsche's top tip

Values are at the heart of branding – but in a much more potent sense than we normally assume. Brand values should not just be 'attachments' to a product or service, but rather the driving force for what the brand can dare to become. Competitive edge lies in creating new values – perhaps risky values – rather than repackaging existing market values. The way to 'superbrands' is through owning the territory that goes with those values.

Wittgenstein's top tip

Don't limit growth by thinking of a brand as 'standing for' one thing in the same way that a picture delineates a particular place or person. Think of your brand as a 'tool' that can, and should, have several uses and applications. A brand does not have only one 'meaning'. A brand's meaning is the combination of *all* its uses and values. The management of 'meaning' in this sense is the essence of modern brand management.

Existentialism's top tip

Avoid the temptation to be swept along by processes, systems, and 'the way we do it here'. Each brand is an individual entity that exists in its own right. If it *doesn't*, then it isn't really a brand in the full sense of being something with which people can have a relationship. So respect it as an individual, make bold decisions on its behalf – and create enough space for it to express itself in new, impactful (and sometimes surprising) ways.

Popper's top tip

Stop thinking in terms of certainties. They do not exist. You should always be looking to replace current ways of thinking with newer, better ones. Criticism is therefore where progress begins. The key is to see brand development in terms of continuous problem solving.